Prai

"Of all our freedoms, religious freedom is the most precious—and in our day, the most endangered. The Liberty Threat awakens the reader to the dangers, explains how we got here, and most importantly, suggests what we must do to preserve and strengthen religious liberty in America."

—Most Rev. Paul S. Loverde, Bishop of Arlington

"In an era that will be defined by repeated assaults on religious liberty, this is a must-read for Americans of faith--and for any American who believes in real liberty. With his engaging, fast-moving style, Jim Tonkowich serves as a most capable guide to the history of religious liberty, covering all the key events and issues, from Nero's violent persecution of Christians to Barack Obama's bloodless but equally insidious policies. Are you worried about the present and future attacks on religion and liberty? Read this—and then don't forget to follow the proposed solutions."

—Dr. Kevin Roberts, President, Wyoming Catholic College

"The threat to our consciences today is so severe that citizens of all social, political and educational levels will need to get into the fight. The number of Christians being beaten, raped and killed each year is the highest in history. On a far lower scale, even here in the United States, the climate is becoming more hostile to Christians than ever before. . . . For those who want a readable account of the turbulent history of religious liberty both in its high and its low moments, and not written as a college textbook, this book will be very satisfying.

—Amb. Michael Novak, retired George Frederick Jewett Scholar in Religion, Philosophy, and Public Policy from the American Enterprise Institute, visiting professor at Ave Maria University.

"A targeted practical study of religious liberty informed by Christian hope with helpful resources, excellent for parish groups and adult education."

This little book will take its place as one of the best surveys of religious liberty American style—what it is, where it came from, and why it is in crisis—on the market today. Written in the rich, punchy style of Kevin Hasson's The Right to Be Wrong, James Tonkowich's The Liberty Threat surveys the historical and contemporary evidence in a masterful fashion. From the early Church fathers to the American founding and beyond, Tonkowich writes with authority and verve. Read this book. Wherever you stand on the greatest issue of our day—the meaning and value of religious freedom—you won't be disappointed.

"The Liberty Threat is a welcome overview of the challenges to religious liberty that America faces. Written by a layman, it is a great introduction to one of the most pressing issues of our day. People of all faiths will find it a useful resource."

"Jim Tonkowich has written a brilliant, eloquent defense of religious liberty, and perhaps the very best book on the topic of our era. He has an eloquent pen and sterling, fluid style. James Madison, the principal architect of our Constitution, wrote religious liberty was our most sacred property right, that without it, our other freedoms weren't secure either. Tonkowich's excellent book is worthy of Madison, and it could not be more timely or relevant for the fulsome national debate we are having on religious liberty in America."

THE
LIBERTY
THREAT

THE
LIBERTY
THREAT

THE ATTACK ON RELIGIOUS
FREEDOM IN AMERICA TODAY

James Tonkowich

SAINT BENEDICT + PRESS

Charlotte, North Carolina

Cataloging-in-Publication data on file with the Library of Congress

Typeset by Lapiz

Cover artwork and design by Milo Persic

ISBN: 978-1-61890-641-0

Published in the United States by
Saint Benedict Press, LLC
PO Box 410487
Charlotte, NC 28241
www.SaintBenedictPress.com

Printed and bound in the United States of America

To my brother, Greg Tonkowich
1956–2014

About the Author

Dr. James Tonkowich is a freelance writer, speaker, and commentator on religion and public life. A weekly columnist at ChristianHeadlines.com, he has contributed to a wide variety of opinion sites and publications. He also serves as Special Advisor to the President for Strategic Initiatives at Wyoming Catholic College.

Contents

Prologue

RELIGIOUS LIBERTY has been one of the defining characteristics of the United States. When the American founders enumerated our rights as citizens, religious liberty came first before freedom of speech, of press, of assembly, and of petition. Religious liberty is central to who we are as a people.

While the implementation of religious liberty in America has never been perfect, nearly two hundred twenty-five years after the Bill of Rights our religious liberty is under unprecedented attack. Small business owners, academics, religious leaders, veterans groups, military personnel, school children, university students, and countless others have been told that their religious convictions are not protected under the law, must be hidden lest they offend, and are little more than irrational prejudices that can and must be ignored in the important moral and political debates of our era.

Some will say, "That can't happen here. This is America." But it can happen here and, worse yet, it has been happening here for years.

In the Old Testament, men from the tribe of Issachar, we are told, "were endowed with an understanding of the times and who knew what Israel had to do" (1 Chronicles 12:33).

This book is written so that Christian people today might understand the times—this era, which God has entrusted to us—and know what to do.

While this book is about religious liberty in the United States, it's impossible to understand where we are and where we're going without understanding where we've been.

Where did religious liberty come from? Who "discovered" it? And, given the history, how has the Church understood religious liberty?

To answer those questions, we need to go back to early Church history where we find the ancient Christian roots of modern religious liberty. We'll do that in chapter 1.

Chapter 2 takes us from the Pilgrims' landing on Plymouth Rock through the ratification of the U. S. Constitution. In Chapter 3, we'll look at the ways in which religious liberty has always been problematic from the early 1800s through about 1950.

Chapter 4 looks at the threats to religious liberty today and Chapter 5 suggests ways in which we can respond.

CHAPTER ONE

The Ancient Christian Roots of Modern Religious Liberty

Just a Pinch of Incense

IT really didn't seem like a big deal to most people. Just take a pinch of incense and offer it to the Roman gods. It was simple, it took very little time, and making the sacrifice marked you as a person of good standing in the community, a civic minded individual. Besides, the consequences of not performing this seemingly trivial rite of worship were exile, prison, beatings, torture, or even death.

After a simple risk/reward analysis, many Christians in third century Carthage in Roman North Africa chose to avoid legal hassles, made the prescribed sacrifice, and received a certificate of compliance. Many of the Christians, but not all. Their bishop, Thascius Cyprianus who we know as St. Cyprian, reasoned that those who offered a sacrifice, however minute and insincere, to the Roman gods committed the sin of idolatry, for they had, he said, "broken their oath to Christ."

On August 30th, 257 AD, Cyprian was called before Paternus, the Roman proconsul. "The most sacred Emperors Valerian and Gallienus have honored me with letters," he told Cyprian, "wherein they enjoin that all those who use not the religion of Rome, shall formally make profession of their return to the use of the Roman rites; I have made accordingly enquiry of your name; what answer do you make to me?"

"I am a Christian and Bishop," replied Cyprian, "I know no other gods besides the One and true God, who made heaven and earth, the sea, and all things therein; this God we Christians serve, to Him we pray day and night, for ourselves, for all mankind, for the health of the Emperors themselves."[1] As to offering sacrifices to Roman gods, Cyprian refused and Paternus sent him into exile.

A year later, Cyprian was recalled to face another trial before the new proconsul, Galerus Maximus. "The most sacred Emperors have commanded you to conform to the Roman rites," Galerus insisted. Cyprian again refused, but this time there would be no exile. Galerius announced:

You have long lived an irreligious life, and have drawn together a number of men bound by an unlawful association, and professed yourself an open enemy to the gods and the religion of Rome; and the pious, most sacred, and august Emperors, Valerian and Gallienus, and the most noble Cæsar Valerian, have endeavored in vain to bring you back to conformity with their religious observances; whereas then you have been apprehended as principal and ringleader in these infamous crimes, you shall be made an example to those whom you have wickedly associated with you: the authority of law shall be ratified in your blood. It is the will of this court, that Thascius Cyprianus be promptly beheaded.[2]

Cyprian was promptly taken to a nearby field where he removed his cloak, spread it on the ground, and knelt in prayer. After being blindfolded, the executioner swung his sword and "blessed Cyprian went to his death, and his body was laid out nearby to satisfy the curiosity of the pagans."

That night, the Christians carried him away and buried him "with prayers and great pomp, with wax tapers and funeral torches." His feast day is September 16.

Religious Conformity

As the story of St. Cyprian's martyrdom illustrates, religious freedom was rare in the ancient world. If you were an Israelite, you worshiped the LORD God. If you were a Canaanite, you worshipped Baal. If you were an Amorite, you worshipped Molech. If you lived in Babylon in the sixth century BC, you were warned that "when you hear the sound of the horn, pipe, zither, dulcimer, harp, double-flute, and all the other musical instruments, you must fall down and worship the golden statue which King Nebuchadnezzar has set up." If you refused to worship the king's god? "Whoever does not fall down and worship shall be instantly cast into a white-hot furnace," and as Shadrach, Meshach, and Abednego discovered, this was no idle threat (Daniel 3:1-23).

If you lived in the Roman Empire as the early Christians did, you were expected to worship the gods of Rome, including "the Divine Caesar," that is, the emperor. The Romans saw religion as the force that bound family members to one another and people to their ruler. Thus worshiping the gods was central to family, civic, and political life, invoking the blessing of the gods on family, emperor, and empire. Refusing to sacrifice was irreligious and treasonous.

Of course people in the ancient world felt free to worship gods in addition to their family and national deities. Religious cults and "mystery religions" were enormously popular in Rome, making syncretism the norm. Religious toleration and freedom of worship were extended to those who added gods to the official pantheon, but there was no religious liberty to follow one's conscience and disregard the gods of Rome.

"Hating the Human Race"

The Jewish people were, however, an exception. The Romans, like the Greeks before them, tried to dislodge the Jews' exclusive monotheism, but the Babylonian Captivity had taught them the lesson God intended: syncretism is *not* an option. "Hear, O Israel!" Moses told them centuries earlier, "The LORD is our God, the LORD alone!" (Deuteronomy 6:4). They believed it and had defended it with their lives.

So to prevent unrest and rebellion in Judea, the Romans gave the Jews a pass on paying homage to Jupiter, Hera, Aphrodite, and the rest. At the same time, they never trusted the Jews and more than once subjected them to persecution.

When Christianity came on the scene, the Romans gave it a pass as a sect of Judaism. In about 60 AD, while discussing St. Paul's imprisonment and trial, Roman Governor Festus told King Agrippa that Paul's accusers "had some issues with him about their own religion and about a certain Jesus who had died but who Paul claimed was alive" (Acts 25:19). Christianity appeared to be a new twist on an old, tedious, but tolerated religion.

Then in 64 AD, a fire raged through Rome, burning three quarters of the city. The people blamed the emperor, Nero, for starting the fire to clear out a section of the city for his new palace. In truth, he probably didn't start the fire and probably wasn't playing the lyre ("fiddling") as Rome burned, but he did have a political problem.

What Nero needed was a scapegoat, and Christians were the obvious choice. They were an unpopular minority and were badly misunderstood. Christians spoke about eating body and blood and were suspected of cannibalism. They called each other "brother" and "sister," which sounded like incest. They avoided most social interaction and everyone knew they had secrets. Added to that, Christians didn't worship the Roman gods, which made the secretive, incestuous cannibals look seditious as well. In fact, the Roman historian Tacitus wrote that when persecution of Christians began, "a vast multitude were convicted, not so much on the charge of burning the city, as of 'hating the human race.'"

St. Peter, the first pope, was martyred during the persecution. His next thirty-one successors—all the popes until 314 AD—were also martyred.

Nero's persecution, though vicious and cruel, was localized in and around the city of Rome and only lasted four years (64-68 AD). Nonetheless it was a preview of things to come. For two hundred and fifty years, Christians lived with uncertainty at the whim of one government or another as waves of persecution and toleration washed back and forth over cities, provinces, and the Empire as a whole.

Today many of the world's Christians live with the same uncertainty. We may be among them.

Religious Liberty is Born

In the face of persecution early in the third century, the Christian theologian and apologist Tertullian wrote a letter to Scapula, the proconsul at Carthage. In his letter, Tertullian presented a new idea in a world of religious conformity and coercion. Tertullian introduced the world to religious liberty.

"We are worshippers of one God," he told Scapula. "You think that others, too, are gods, whom we know to be devils." (Tact was apparently not Tertullian's strong suit.) In light of those religious differences, he went on to say:

> . . . it is a fundamental human right, a privilege of nature, that every man should worship according to his own convictions: one man's religion neither harms nor helps another man. It is assuredly no part of religion to compel religion—to which free will and not force should lead us—the sacrificial victims even being required of a willing mind. You will render no real service to your gods by compelling us to sacrifice. For they can have no desire of offerings from the unwilling, unless they are animated by a spirit of contention, which is a thing altogether undivine.[3]

Rome, argued Tertullian, got everything wrong. Rome was wrong about the nature of man. They had the idea that the state was supposed to control people's religion, turning persecution or toleration on and off at will. Instead, he argued, religious liberty precedes even the state being "a fundamental human right, a privilege of nature." This means that every human being is owed the freedom to believe or not believe as he or she pleases on the basis of being a part of the human race. This was by far Tertullian's most important insight.

Rome was also wrong about the nature of religion. Romans believed forced sacrifices and, thus, insincere worship were in some way pleasing to the gods and helped the cause of religion and Empire. On the contrary, said Tertullian, coerced worship is no worship at all, but a mockery. "It is assuredly no part of religion to compel religion—to which free will and not force should lead us. . . ."

And Rome was also wrong about the nature of their gods. The gods (if they were really gods) can tell whether someone worships out of sincere faith or insincere conformity. Real gods, he wrote, "can have no desire of offerings from the unwilling, unless they are animated by a spirit of contention," which would mean that they are not gods at all.

Rome thought ignoring the gods was a threat to family and empire. But unless religious beliefs constitute a clear and present danger, ("picks my pocket" or "breaks my leg" to use Thomas Jefferson's words)[4], "one man's religion neither harms nor helps another man." The only solution, Tertullian reasoned, is what we call religious liberty.

(Having mentioned Thomas Jefferson, let me add that Jefferson, who we'll take up in chapter 2, read Tertullian and agreed.)

Good News from Milan

Nearly a century after the death of Tertullian, Lucius Lactantius expressed similar ideas. The difference was that while Tertullian was trying to get the ear of a proconsul, Lactantius had the ear of the emperor, Constantine.

"Religion," he wrote, "is to be defended not by putting to death, but by dying, not by cruelty but by patience, not by an impious act but by faith. . . . For if you wish to defend religion by bloodshed, and by tortures, and by doing evil, it will not be defended but polluted and profaned. For nothing is so much a matter of free will as religion. . . ."[5]

Not only must true religion be free, it must be believed from the heart: "For how will God love the worshipper if He Himself is not loved by him, or grant the petitioner whatever he asks when he draws near and offers his prayer without sincerity or reverence?"[6]

Forcing Christians who did not believe in the Roman gods to offer sacrifices was an exercise in futility. The gods, assuming they existed at all, would not have been pleased with the sacrifice and could have possibly been angered at the lack of sincerity and reverence.

Stamping out Christianity by force has never been an option because Christ is building his Church and, as he said, "the gates of the netherworld shall not prevail against it" (Matthew 16:18). Many tried, including Emperor Diocletian (284–305 AD) who unleashed a vicious, empire-wide persecution of Christians. It didn't work and by Constantine's time, the impossibility of getting rid of the Church was clear even to most politicians.

The time had come for a new religious policy in the Empire, now divided between two emperors. So Western Emperor Constantine, a Christian (or at least pro-Christian) and Eastern Emperor Licinius, a pagan, issued the Edict of Milan in 313 AD. While the edict did not make Christianity "the official religion of the Roman Empire," as some erroneously believe, it did something that in the long run was even more significant. The edict gave all people in the Roman Empire religious liberty, something that was unprecedented in the ancient world and is still rare today.

In the edict, Constantine and Licinus granted "to the Christians and others full authority to observe that religion which each preferred. . . ." As of the edict anyone "who wishes to observe the Christian religion may do so freely and openly, without molestation."[7]

Christian property, seized in persecutions, had to be restored to individuals and to churches. Christians could lawfully worship, evangelize, and live according to the dictates of their faith. Churches could lawfully assemble, own property, and conduct their own business unmolested.

And not only Christians would benefit. The edict explicitly allowed "other religions the right of open and free observance of their worship for the sake of the peace of our times, that each one may have the free opportunity to worship as he pleases; this regulation is made that we may not seem to detract from any dignity or any religion."[8]

Pagans who did not believe in Christ would not be forced into the Church, because coercion can never bring about "a sincere and pure commitment to Christ" (2 Corinthians 11:3) in the heart of an unbeliever.

Now it's true that this bright supernova of freedom didn't last. Licinius went back to the East and reneged on the edict. Christians, sad to say, once they had the upper hand politically, engaged in the sporadic persecution of pagans. And within fifty years, Emperor Julian (the Apostate) renewed the persecution of Christians across the Roman Empire in paganism's last gasp.

Our First Freedom

Nonetheless religious liberty was now part of the record. As a result human freedom took a quantum leap forward with the Edict of Milan because religious liberty is the foundation of all our liberties. It is our first freedom: first in order and first in importance.

Consider: if you have "freedom of speech," but aren't allowed to articulate your most deeply held religious beliefs, how free to speak are you really? You are not free at all. Freedom of speech without religious freedom is hollow and meaningless.

Similarly freedom of assembly is not free if you can't assemble over the truths that are most dear to you. Freedom to petition the government does us no good if we can only petition the government for things that have nothing to do with our faith. Traffic laws or banking regulations might be okay topics for petition, but not issues of life or marriage or war or the poor if our positions come out of our religious convictions.

The Edict of Milan granted religious liberty, not "religious toleration" or "freedom of worship." Both of those are, in effect, permission for privately held and privately practiced beliefs, that is, religion as hobby, a way to spend your free time on Sunday. Religious liberty, by contrast, is the freedom to speak, assemble, advocate, and act in accord with the dictates of conscience.

And remember, this first freedom, the *sine qua non* of all of our freedoms, is a Christian idea advanced in the face of persecution, prison, and martyrdom. The Church through history has, (with some notable stumbles) continued to advance religious liberty, using the same arguments made by Tertullian and Lactantius.

Religious Liberty and Christendom

But what, someone will ask, about the Middle Ages, the Counter-Reformation, and the Spanish Inquisition? Didn't the Church enlist the coercive power of the state against people it considered heretics? And didn't thinkers like Thomas Aquinas, Robert Bellarmine, and Francisco Suárez argue that the Church had a right—even a duty—to crush opposition because "error has no rights"? Did religious freedom just evaporate?

Good questions. The answers revolve around the rise of Christendom in Europe.

In the Roman Empire, Christians were a minority, but by the Middle Ages, they were the overwhelming majority. Nearly everyone in Europe was a baptized member of the Catholic Church, and that changed their status *vis-à-vis* religious liberty.

When we received the sacrament of baptism, either we made vows or our godparents made vows for us, vows that bind us forever. As a result, once we are baptized, the Church has not so much the right as the responsibility to help us fulfill our vows and so attain Heaven, and guard us from breaking our vows and suffering the penalty of Hell.

We see this in 1 Corinthians 5:1-8. A Christian man in Corinth was openly having relations with his stepmother, something so immoral, wrote St. Paul, that it is "not found even among pagans."

What was at stake? First, the honor and glory of God were at stake. Pagans would look in horror at the Church as an immoral group with a presumably immoral God. Second, the life of the church was at stake. Behavioral norms in any community spread. If sleeping with stepmom is okay for one, it's okay for all. Over time the man's salvation was at stake. Without correction, he would die in his sin to face judgment and condemnation.

So out of love for the honor and glory of God, love for the Church and its members, and love for the man in danger of Hell, St. Paul wrote, "[W]hen you have gathered together and I am with you in spirit with the power of the Lord Jesus, you are to deliver this man to Satan for the destruction of his flesh, so that his spirit may be saved on the day of the Lord."

St. Paul ordered excommunication, not to destroy the man, but for his benefit and the Church's benefit. Paul intended that the discipline would result in repentance— a changed heart and changed behavior—and it did (See 2 Corinthians 2:5-11).

What about the man's religious liberty? He had the freedom to be baptized or not. He chose baptism and (we presume, freely) pledged himself to the Lord Jesus Christ and his Church. And while the baptized still have religious liberty politically, spiritually we are bound to the Church and her teachings. The state may not coerce us, but in our baptism we've given the Church permission to do just that.

So in Medieval Europe when almost everyone was baptized, the Jesuit theologian Francisco Suárez argued, "But in truth the baptized are under an obligation both to God and the Church by reason of baptism, and therefore can specifically be compelled by the Church to remain in the faith or to return to it." In this sense, in spite of being ill-treated, Jews and Muslims in Christendom Europe had greater religious freedom than baptized Christians who were (and are) subject to the Church.

Persecution and Pluralism

Christendom, however, didn't last. In the sixteenth century, the unthinkable happened as great swaths of the Catholic Church re-formed into Lutherans, Calvinists, Anglicans, Anabaptists, and assorted others. Yes, all were baptized and so, on some level, were still under the jurisdiction of the Catholic (Universal) Church, but on a practical level, everything was different. Christendom was over.

But the *idea* of Christendom was not over. After theological statements, popular rebellions, and outright wars, the Peace of Augsburg (1555) decided *Cuius regio, eius religio,* "Whose realm, his religion." If your prince was Lutheran, you were Lutheran. This just split Christendom into smaller units with the added problem that refusal to adhere to your ruler's religion was taken not just as a theological error, but as treason.

While England was not party to the Peace of Augsburg, Elizabeth I imposed Protestantism on her unwilling Catholic populace by uniting worship in the Church of England with patriotism. Catholics, Puritans, Quakers, and others were persecuted in England less for their theology than for their disloyalty to the crown. This would then have implications for the American colonies, as we will see.

Eventually, however, even the idea of Christendom died. It had to. A shattered Church became a fact of life. The rise of religious freedom beginning in the United States created pluralism. And the secularism and anti-Christian biases of Revolutionary France, Civil War Spain, Nazi Germany, and Communist Eastern Europe put Christians on the defensive and renewed the days of persecution and martyrdom.

Against this background, the Second Vatican Council issued its Declaration on Religious Freedom, *Dignitatis Humanae.*

While there were those who would like to think the Church has changed her position on religious liberty, *Dignitatis Humanae* is a reaffirmation of what the Church has always taught. In it are echoes of Tertullian, Lactantius, and Suárez:

> Religious freedom . . . which men demand as necessary to fulfill their duty to worship God, has to do with immunity from coercion in civil society. [Tertullian/Lactantius] Therefore it leaves untouched traditional Catholic doctrine on the moral duty of men and societies toward the true religion and toward the one Church of Christ. [Suárez][9]

Dignitatis Humanae argues along with Tertullian's great insight that religious liberty is rooted in human nature. Because abridging religious liberty violates our human dignity, religious liberty must be protected by constitutional means everywhere in the world. Individuals and communities should be immune from coercion in matters of religion. Families have the right to raise their children in their faith and "the right of parents are violated, if their children are forced to attend lessons or instructions which are not in agreement with their religious beliefs, or if a single system of education, from which all religious formation is excluded, is imposed upon all".[10]

Just as individuals may not be coerced, so the Church has a right to freedom from coercion. She is independent and is free in matters of doctrine, leadership, evangelization, and authority over the faithful.

The Council made it clear that it was not just talking about privatized faith, that is, religious toleration or freedom of worship. The Council Fathers declared, "the Christian faithful, in common with all other men, possess the civil right not to be hindered in leading lives in accordance with their consciences."

It is this religious liberty that is under threat in America today.

Conclusion

Many people believe that Christians—particularly the Catholic Church—hate liberty and are doing whatever is possible to shrink our human freedom. As it turns out, they couldn't be more wrong. Christians have, it's true, been against the false freedom of anything-goes libertinism and we have from time to time broken our own rules by violation the religious freedom of others. But at the same time, we invented religious liberty and with it generated all the other freedoms we enjoy as well.

Defending religious liberty in the twenty-first century makes us a part of the Church's heritage of freedom. In that, like the Church Fathers and the Vatican II Fathers, we need to insist on religious liberty for all. As the late Richard John Neuhaus said we seek neither a secular "naked" public square nor a Christian "religious" public square, but a civil public square. And it's in that civil public square that we must be free to propose, not impose, the Christian story as the truth about the world and about humans.

This vision is in keeping with another set of fathers: the American Founding Fathers whose story comprises the next chapter.

CHAPTER TWO

Sweet Land of Liberty: From the Pilgrims to the Constitution

ASK almost anyone and he or she will tell you that the Pilgrims set sail on the Mayflower in 1620 because they wanted religious liberty. England had an established state church, the Church of England. These dissenters wanted to live according to the dictates of conscience, dictates that differed from the Church of England's mandated theology, worship, and practice.

And that's all true, with one caveat: while the Pilgrims wanted religious liberty for themselves, they had no interest whatsoever in extending religious liberty to anyone else. That took years of thought, discord, and suffering before the now-independent states ratified the Constitution and with it the Bill of Rights. Even religious toleration is a long way from the religious liberty guaranteed by the First Amendment: "Congress shall make no law respecting an establishment of religion, or prohibiting the free exercise thereof."

17

The story of how we got from Plymouth Rock to the Constitution is crucial for understanding what the American founders had in mind when they wrote the First Amendment, the conflicts that almost immediately cropped up over church and state, and the threats we're living with today.

The Revenge of Christendom

The Pilgrims were one sect among the English Puritans in the late sixteenth and early seventeenth centuries. While all the various Puritan groups were slightly different, all had a common goal. The Puritans, influenced by Reformation theologian John Calvin, believed that the Church of England was insufficiently reformed. The Bible and therefore God demanded more changes than the so-called Elizabethan Settlement granted. The Church in England needed to be purified and they believed that they were the ones chosen for the job.

To bring about reform, many Puritans remained Anglicans, loyal members of the Church of England who sought to influence the church's future from within. This had the added advantage of avoiding the weekly fine levied on anyone who refused to attend approved worship services. Others—fine or no fine—rejected the state church with its bishops, prayer book, candles, robes, chalices, holy days, and assorted other things they considered refuse from England's "papist" past. These separatists set up their own churches.

Their rejection of the Church of England, however, was not a principled rejection of state churches in general. In the seventeenth century, the only paradigm anyone had for the relationship of church and state was the Christendom paradigm discussed in the last chapter. *Cuius regio, eius religio,* "Whose realm, his religion" was part of the air everyone breathed.

The kind of robust religious liberty proposed by Tertullian and Lactantius and mandated in the Edict of Milan had, over the course of 1,200 years, vanished from the Christian West's collective memory.

The group of Puritans who we call the Pilgrims were a particularly fussy and cantankerous group of separatists. They utterly rejected the Church of England and all its "Romish" practices, and chose to move to Holland in the early 1600s, presumably knocking the dust off their boots in the process. Holland was, after all, a Calvinist country that afforded them the liberty to believe and to live out their faith as they chose, even if the Dutch Calvinists didn't agree with them on every jot and tittle.

The move seemed as though it should have been a good choice, but after a few years the Pilgrims realized they had blundered.

In Holland, not only did their children begin speaking Dutch, but also some of the sharp Pilgrim distinctives started to get rounded off from their interactions with their less pure (from their point of view) Calvinist neighbors. In Holland they had freedom, but not separation from everything they considered theological and moral error. There they realized that the kind of separation they sought wouldn't happen unless they were in charge of the state. That would require a new world, or rather, *the* New World,

The Pilgrims packed up in Holland and moved back to England. Then in the summer of 1620, the Mayflower set sail carrying both the Pilgrims (the "saints") and others (the "strangers"). The strangers, who were in the minority, didn't share the Pilgrims faith or mission. They had personal and economic reasons for undertaking the voyage and didn't share the Pilgrim's brand of Christianity.

Upon arrival in Plymouth the Pilgrims were finally free to do things their way, setting up a government and a church they considered pure, unsullied, and utterly biblical. Then, by law, they coerced everyone including the strangers to attend their church and live according to their rules. What about those with religious differences? Too bad for them. The Pilgrims were finally the majority. That gave them the power to force their religion on everyone, so that's what they did.

When the financial backers of the Plymouth Colony sent Church of England minister John Lyford to the colony in 1624, he, as anyone would expect, set up an Anglican church. The Pilgrim leadership promptly banished him. They would tolerate no religious competition. When Quakers—the Pilgrims' theological cousins—sent representatives to Massachusetts, they were beaten, imprisoned, and banished. The ones who returned received even worse treatment including having their tongues cut out, merciless and prolonged beatings, or execution. The Quakers were, after all, wrong, and both church and state were empowered to silence them.

A Providential Banishment

Despite the best efforts of the Pilgrims and other Puritans in the Massachusetts Bay Colony, people with differing religious ideas kept on showing up, including a young man named Roger Williams.

Williams had studied for the ministry at Cambridge University and, when he first arrived in Boston in 1631, people were so impressed with him that they offered him a teaching position at the most prestigious church in town. Sorry, said Williams. The Boston church, he observed, never officially condemned the Church of England as heretical and so it wasn't pure enough. Williams then left Boston for Salem, Massachusetts. After being disappointed with the purity of churches in Salem, he went south to Plymouth. There too he found impurity and, rejecting even the Pilgrims, he trudged back to Boston.

Williams, needless to say, earned himself a reputation as a malcontent and a troublemaker. Nonetheless the authorities put up with him until one of his rants sent them over the top. Williams argued that civil authorities should have no say whatsoever in religious matters. The state, he said, is responsible for the wellbeing of our bodies, not our souls. Therefore, the state should never interfere with church matters. Williams even went so far as to compare state enforced religion to rape.

In his treatise on religious liberty, *The Bloody Tenent of Persecution for Cause of Conscience,* Williams quoted, among others, Tertullian. But where Tertullian grounded religious liberty in human nature, Williams grounded it in the nature of God. God, he said, wants us to be free and rejects religious coercion. We must do the same.

The leadership of the Massachusetts Bay Colony, where church and state were joined at the hip, begged to differ. They believed that not only did God permit the state to coerce religion, he commanded it. Before the authorities could arrest Williams and his followers they fled south to establish the colony of Providence in Rhode Island.

In a 1654 letter to the people of Providence, Williams compared their town to a ship. Passengers on a ship may be "papists and Protestants, Jews and Turks [Muslims]." While each must pay the fare and all are subject to the ship's master and crew for safety and physical wellbeing, he insisted that none "be forced to come to the ship's prayers or worship, nor compelled from their own particular prayers or worship, if they practice any."[1] As it is on a ship, so it should be in any commonwealth. This was a new thought for that era.

With the founding of Providence, religious liberty of a sort not seen in the West for perhaps a millennium took root on the shore of Narragansett Bay. Despite the exclusion of some groups—atheists and Catholics being at the top of the list—in 1658 Touro Synagogue, the first in North America, was founded in Rhode Island.

A Land for Mary

Further south on the shores of the Chesapeake Bay another experiment in religious freedom was launched.

George Calvert, First Lord Baltimore, had been, prior to his conversion to Catholicism, a senior official in the court of England's King Charles I. The king of England was, of course, head of the Church of England. Nonetheless, Calvert managed to negotiate Charles' marriage to the Catholic French Princess Henrietta Maria, who, even as Queen of England, enjoyed what Calvert called "free exercise" of religion.

(That's right, the phrase "free exercise" that wound up in our Constitution originally came from a Catholic.)

Calvert also believed that such free exercise should apply not only to the Queen and her court. It should extend to everyone, and so he secured from the king a royal charter. He named the colony, with a nod to the queen and a deep bow to Our Lady, Maryland.

Maryland as founded included free exercise in the form of religious toleration. The 1649 "Toleration Act" passed by Maryland's colonial legislature states that:

> ... no person or persons whatsoever within this province, or the islands, ports, harbors, creeks, or havens thereunto belonging, professing to believe in Jesus Christ, shall from henceforth be in any way troubled, molested, or discountenanced for or in respect of his or her religion, nor in the free exercise thereof within this province or the islands thereunto belonging, nor in any way compelled to the belief or exercise of any other religion against his or her consent, so as they be not unfaithful to the Lord Proprietary, or molest or conspire against the civil government established or to be established in this province under him or his heirs.

Note three things. First, the bad news: this is toleration, not religious liberty. Free exercise was reserved for Christians. Jews, atheists, Muslims, and other non-Christians received none. Second, the good news: free exercise was for all Christians. Maryland would, to use the language of the Bill of Rights, make "no law respecting an establishment of religion, or prohibiting the free exercise thereof" at least for

Christians. Third, the act sees religious toleration as a means to ensure tranquility. Europe was at war over religion because of religious coercion. Maryland would be at peace because of religious toleration.

That third point was way ahead of its time. Commenting on religious liberty in our world today, scholars Monica Duffy Toft, Daniel Philpott, and Timothy Shah write in their book *God's Century: Resurgent Religion and Global Politics* that we must, "Accept that if governments fail to respect the institutional independence of religious actors, especially through systematic repression, . . . these governments will encourage pathological forms of religious politics, including religion-based terrorism and religion-related civil wars."[2] That is, religious coercion breeds radicalism and violence while religious liberty contributes to civil tranquility.

So far so good, but Maryland, in addition to being an example of the good of religious toleration, is also an example of its limits. Religious toleration contains a fatal flaw.

In 1654, just five years after the Toleration Act, politics in Maryland shifted and the legislature ended up with a Protestant majority. That majority promptly repealed the Toleration Act. A year later, ten Catholics were sentenced to death and four were actually executed for their faith. By 1692, Maryland's religion was officially Anglicanism and Catholics became a suspicious minority.

In his book *The Right to Be Wrong*, Kevin Seamus Hasson explains that what went wrong with religious toleration in Maryland was what always goes wrong with religious toleration.

The authority to choose to tolerate presumes the authority *not* to tolerate. Any government that thinks it is being generous, or shrewd, or pragmatic to put up with dissent faiths necessarily believes it has the power to persecute them if circumstances change. Tolerance, in short, is just a policy choice of the government, not a right of the people. And policy choices can be reversed.[3]

Religious liberty, as Tertullian understood, is a the gift from God. We possess it because we are human. In marked contrast, religious toleration is not a gift of God, but the gift of the government, and what the government gives, the government can take. Religious liberty is carved into the bedrock of natural law. Religious toleration is always written in sand.

Meanwhile Back in England

The plight of religion in English Colonies was largely a function of the religious scene at home, which was, in turn, tied to the English monarchy. And during the seventeenth century, England, the monarchy, and religion were in almost constant turmoil.

Queen Elizabeth I reigned from 1558 to 1603 and established the Protestant Church of England, and you would have thought the religious hullabaloo was over. It might have been except that Elizabeth died childless and the throne went to her cousin, James I (to whom the King James Bible was dedicated).

James was succeeded by his son, Charles I, in 1625. Charles, as the "Supreme Head of the Church of England", committed the nearly unforgivable sin of marrying a French Catholic. On top of that, there is evidence that Charles himself was secretly Catholic. His reign was deeply troubled and riddled with religious and political controversies. It ended abruptly in 1649 when Puritans under the command of Oliver Cromwell took control of the country and executed him.

The queen and her sons, the future Charles II and James II, fled to Catholic France. After the Puritan Commonwealth collapsed in 1660, England happily welcomed back monarchy and Charles II. Charles wasn't very interested in religion, preferring hunting, the theater, and wenching. But he nonetheless had to deal with the aftermath of the Puritan debacle and the ongoing anti-Catholicism. To his credit, he tried to offer religious toleration to both separatist Protestants and to Catholics.

James II, who succeeded his brother in 1685, was a different story. James married a Catholic and made no attempt to hide his own Catholic faith. It looked as though England would once again have a Catholic monarchy in spite of Henry VIII and contemporary objections. But when James attempted to promote the Catholic faith, he made more enemies than he knew what to do with.

At the urging of some of James' subjects, James' distant German cousin William of Orange invaded in 1688. Yes, there were problems with a German king of England, but William was a dyed-in-the-wool, card-carrying Protestant. He and his Protestant wife, Mary, were welcomed while James fled to France.

A year later, parliament passed the Toleration Act of 1689 that required all persons to swear:

> I, [your name] do sincerely promise and solemnly declare before God and the world, that I will be true and faithful to King William and Queen Mary; and I do solemnly profess and declare, that I do from my heart abhor, detest, and renounce, as impious and heretical, that damnable doctrine and position, that princes excommunicated or deprived by the Pope, or any authority of the See of Rome, may be deposed or murdered by their subjects, or any other whatsoever. And I do declare, that no foreign prince, person, prelate, state, or potentate, hath or ought to have, any power, jurisdiction, superiority, pre-eminence, or authority ecclesiastical or spiritual within this realm.

> I, [your name] profess faith in God the Father, and in Jesus Christ His eternal Son, the true God, and in the Holy Spirit, one God blessed for evermore, and do acknowledge the Holy Scriptures of the Old and New Testament to be given by divine inspiration.[4]

The so-called "Glorious Revolution" established Anglicanism and finalized the Protestant Reformation in England—and her Colonies.

Virginia Tolerates the Baptists

The Toleration Act brought new strength and confidence to the established church in America. Not only did Anglicanism become the established church in Maryland, but it also grew stronger in the colonies where it was already established, in places like Virginia.

Not that the Anglicans didn't tolerate other Christian groups, they did, but they reserved the right to manage and control them. If Baptists, a significant minority in Virginia, wished to preach, they were free to do so. They just had to register with every county in which they wanted to preach by swearing the Toleration Act oath and obtaining a license.

The Baptists argued that their call to preach Christ and their authority to preach his Gospel did not come from the king, the Parliament, or the counties. Their call and authority came from God. Many preachers, therefore, refused to register, choosing instead to risk beatings, fines, and prison.

One such Baptist preacher—but hardly the only one— was Joseph Spencer from Orange County, Virginia. In 1768, Spencer was arrested on charges of preaching without a license. He was admonished to never to preach without a license again, swore a modified version of the Toleration Act oath, and was set free. In 1773, he was arrested for "a Breach of his Good Behaviour in teaching & Preaching The Gospel as a Baptist not having a License."[5]

The court, somewhat impatient with a repeat offender, ordered Spencer to post bail of £100 (about $10,000 today) as a guarantee that he would not preach any more. The money would be forfeit if he did. Spencer either didn't have the money or refused on principle and was tossed into prison. In prison he could have had the right to walk freely about the prison grounds if he put up a bail of £50 (about $5,000). Again he either could not or would not post the bail and was confined to a cell for months.

Next door in Culpepper County, there were at one point six Baptist preachers similarly imprisoned. In a particularly shameful incident, a sheriff accompanied by an Anglican clergyman accosted an unlicensed Baptist preacher as he led an outdoor service. Interrupting him as he sang a hymn, they gagged him with a bullwhip and hauled him off to be publicly flogged.

This toleration of the Baptists serves as a clear illustration of all that is wrong with religious toleration. It puts the government in charge of religion, allowing the state to decide who can preach and what they can legally say. What was needed then and what must be maintained today is religious liberty.

Religious Liberty's Champion

Baptist preachers moldering in prison and worse attracted the attention of a young Virginian named James Madison. He called this sort of toleration just what it was, "that diabolical hell-conceived principle of persecution." Madison had seen enough religious tolerance to know that what was needed was religious *liberty*.

As Madison's biographer Ralph Ketcham noted, "There is no principle in all of Madison's wide range of private opinions and long public career to which he held with greater vigor and tenacity than this one of religious liberty."

For example, while Thomas Jefferson wrote Virginia's Statute for Religious Freedom, under his leadership the bill never got out of committee. Several years later, Madison took charge of the bill and saw to it that it became law.

Madison also guided the fledgling U.S. Congress to adopt the Bill of Rights with its guarantee of religious liberty.

Like Tertullian, Madison reasoned in his *Memorial and Remonstrance Against Religious Assessments*, "The Religion then of every man must be left to the conviction and conscience of every man; and it is the right of every man to exercise it as these may dictate. This right is in its nature an unalienable right." That is, religious liberty arises from our human nature. You and I are the only ones able to decide what we will believe and each of us will be held accountable by God to whom we have a duty.

Because God has a claim on our duty, that duty "is precedent, both in time and in degree of obligation, to the claims of Civil Society." And if religion is beyond the claims of civil society, "still less can it be subject to that of the Legislative Body."

Religious liberty, Madison argued, applies to everyone: "Whilst we assert for ourselves a freedom to embrace, to profess and to observe the Religion which we believe to be of divine origin, we cannot deny an equal freedom to those whose minds have not yet yielded to the evidence which has convinced us."

Beyond this and worst of all, Madison wrote, established religion destroys religion. In most places where religion is established, he noted, it bears the fruit of "pride and indolence in the Clergy, ignorance and servility in the laity, in both, superstition, bigotry and persecution." Instead of establishing religion, he said, America should provide a haven for "the persecuted and oppressed of every Nation and Religion."

Another Champion

Madison's Virginian colleague Thomas Jefferson also worked hard to prevent an established church and guarantee the free exercise of religion. Jefferson had written the Statute for Religious Freedom in Virginia, one of three lifelong accomplishments he ordered written on his tombstone.

Like Madison and Tertullian, Jefferson argued, "Almighty God hath created the mind free." That is, religious liberty is central to our human nature, which, without religious liberty, will become distorted. Attempts to compel religion "by temporal punishments or burdens, or by civil incapacitations, tend only to beget habits of hypocrisy and meanness."

Unlike Madison and Tertullian who believed religious liberty was good for religion, Jefferson believed that in the final analysis religious liberty was bad for religion—and that was just fine with Thomas Jefferson. He longed, in fact, for the day when organized religion would dry up, blow away, and no longer be a bother in the Public Square. He was, in his own words, "a Materialist"[6] who longed for the day when the human race finally advanced beyond religion.

That being said, however, Jefferson favored a sturdy religious liberty and worked hard to make it a characteristic of the American Republic, a Republic where, with the exception of Virginia and New York, each state had established churches and/or religious tests for political office that excluded Catholics, Jews, Muslims, atheists, and others.

Two Short Clauses

When the time came to write a constitution for the newly formed United States, Thomas Jefferson was in Paris and it fell to Madison to do the heavy lifting regarding religious liberty. Politics being, as they say, "the art of the possible," Madison never got the kind of religious liberty he and Jefferson believed in. The First Amendment to the Constitution was a compromise within a compromise.

The Constitution itself contains no references to religious freedom. Nor, for that matter, does it discuss freedom of speech, freedom of the press, or the freedom to bear arms. These are contained in the Bill of Rights that comprises the first ten amendments to the Constitution.

Madison, while he was responsible for the passage of the Bill of Rights, was initially convinced that it was unnecessary. The various freedoms—religious, speech, press, and so on— were, he believed, implicit in the text of the Constitution. Including a supplemental list of rights, he thought, was dangerous. Some important rights might be unwittingly left out and any list could easily be misinterpreted and abused. Such "parchment barriers," are easily breached by majorities and inadequate for describing the full range of natural rights belonging to human beings.

As he and Jefferson exchanged letters, however, Jefferson convinced him to reconsider his position in light of practical political considerations. If the Constitution did not enumerate rights, it was far less likely to be ratified by the states. The state legislatures wanted to know specifically what the federal government could and could not do. The Bill of Rights gave them a list. Jefferson agreed that there were dangers in the Bill of Rights, but wrote to Madison, "half a loaf is better than no bread. If we cannot secure all our rights, let us secure what we can."[7]

Regarding religious liberty, the first statement in the First Amendment reads, "Congress shall make no law respecting an establishment of religion, or prohibiting the free exercise thereof."

Note that the amendment says nothing about what the American people may or may not do. Instead, it restricts what Congress, and with it the federal government, are allowed to do. Congress may not declare a "Church of the United States" to which all good Americans must belong. And Congress may not stop any individual or group from living out their beliefs. These were and are huge concessions of government power, concessions that seem to displease the federal government today.

On the negative side and much to Madison's chagrin, while the amendment restricts Congress, the states maintained their established churches and continued to prohibit the free exercise of religion within their borders. As a result, on a practical level, the amendment changed nothing. Freedom of religion was neither complete nor consistent across the new nation. Most Americans either benefited from or were penalized by state religious toleration laws.

It should be noted that just as freedom of speech does not mean the freedom to commit libel or to stand up in a crowded theater and yell, "Fire!" when there is no fire, so too religious freedom necessarily has restrictions in a civil society. Human sacrifice immediately comes to mind as an extreme example of a religious practice that is rightly banned. But, as we'll discover in the next chapter, from the time the Bill of Rights was added to the Constitution, we Americans have struggled with trying to define the extent of our religious liberty and how limits are to be applied.

CHAPTER THREE

We Hold These Truths

THE threats to our religious liberty today did not pop up out of nowhere. They are instead rooted in American history, and there is no way to understand the times or defend religious liberty without getting a sense of the history out of which our problems arise.

Understand that there has been no American Golden Age of religious freedom. No era of our history has been free of difficulties and controversies. In fact, since the ratification of the Constitution and the Bill of Rights, America has been trying to define exactly what religious liberty should look like in practice. The nineteenth and early twentieth centuries saw the flourishing of religious liberty—for Protestants. Jews were also better off than they had been. But for Mormons, Quakers, and especially for Catholics, it was a time of suspicion and legally established intolerance. And it all, strangely enough, came under the banner of religious liberty and the separation of church and state.

This chapter has two sections. The first looks at the cultural, religious, and political atmosphere of America in the nineteenth and first half of the twentieth centuries. In the second section, we'll explore a few of the many religious liberty cases that have been decided by the Supreme Court. In both sections, we'll focus our attention on one of the centers of controversy: public schools.

The clear conclusion is that religious tolerance—even under the guise of religious liberty—will, sooner or later, strip everyone of this most basic human freedom. We'll also see how the actions of some Christians led directly to the threats all Christians face today.

1. Religion and the Republic

It's a mistake to claim that America was founded as a "Christian" nation. It wasn't. Our founding documents make references to "Nature's God" and to "Providence," not to the Holy Trinity, the God and Father of our Lord Jesus Christ, or our God and Savior Jesus Christ. There was, however, a strong sense that God was the giver of good gifts and in particular the gift of liberty, that he had laid out in the Scriptures the rules of morality and virtue for a free people, that he ruled the world providentially, and that he would one day judge the world and all its inhabitants.

That is, while not founded as a Christian nation, it is certain that America was founded with the assumption that a free people needed religion and not just any religion, but religion in a Judeo-Christian sense of the word.

George Washington, the content of whose faith is notoriously difficult to uncover, spoke for many in his belief

that morality and religion are inseparable: "Let us with cau-
tion indulge the supposition that morality can be maintained
without religion. Reason and experience both forbid us
to expect that national morality can prevail in exclusion of
religious principle."

Washington saw religion as foundational to the American
experiment in ordered liberty: "We are persuaded that good
Christians will always be good citizens, and that where righ-
teousness prevails among individuals the Nation will be great
and happy. Thus while just government protects all in their
religious rights, true religion affords to government it's surest
support."

Washington's successor John Adams famously made this
connection between America's success and our religion: "We
have no government armed with power of contending with
human passions unbridled by morality and religion. Avarice,
ambition, revenge, or gallantry*, would break the strongest
cords of our Constitution as a whale goes through a net. Our
Constitution was made only for a moral and religious people.
It is wholly inadequate to the government of any other."

Even Benjamin Franklin, not a believer or a friend of the
Christian faith, argued that in schools and colleges, religion
should be one of the primary subjects in the curriculum.
Religion, he believed, along with Washington and Adams,
was at the center of character training. Without it, the young
would lack virtue, and the lack of virtue would destroy the
constitutional republic they had worked so hard to establish.

Nowhere can we see this connection between religion
and virtue—in particular civic virtue—than in the founding

---

* Used pejoratively to mean self-centered ostentation and showiness.

of America's "common" or, as we call them today, public
schools.

Religious Awakening and Public Schools

The idea of government-sponsored education for all children
arose in the mid-1800s concomitant with the Second Great
Awakening, a great revival of Protestant piety, zeal, and evangelization. Hundreds of thousands of Americans professed
faith in Christ for the first time or for the first time in a long
time. Christianity was the talk of every city, town, and vil-
lage as traveling evangelists crisscrossed the country leading
revival meetings.

The leading evangelist of the time was Charles Finney.
In reflecting on the revival meetings during the awakening,
Finney, said, "Persons of all denominations, forgetting their
differences, gave themselves to the work. They all preached
the same thing, the same simple Gospel. They held out substantially the same truth: Christ died to save souls; you may
be saved; you are a sinner and need to be saved; now, will you
come to Christ and submit yourself to God? This was about
the amount of instruction."

While the First Great Awakening in the 1740s was, for
the most part, steadfastly Calvinistic, the Second Great
Awakening was broadly Protestant, much like the evangelical movement today. And while the First Awakening
was theologically precise, Finney and others preached "the
same simple Gospel" leaving out what they saw as second-
ary (at best) theological and denominational distinctions.
This was viewed as non-sectarian Christianity and it was

this non-sectarian Christianity that was applied in the public schools.

Historian Paul Johnson in his *A History of the American People* points out that "the true American public school, in accordance with the Constitution, was non-sectarian from the very beginning. Non-sectarian, yes; but not non-religious. What the schools got was not so much non-denominational religion as a kind of lowest-common-denominator Protestantism, based upon the Bible, the Ten Commandments, and such useful tracts as Bunyan's *Pilgrim's Progress*."[1] In this way, the schools provided the type and quantity of Christianity deemed necessary for building civic virtue and character in the students. Parents and churches would add any "sectarian" particulars if they were added at all.

This was all well and good for Protestant children, but in the growing nation of immigrants, not all children were Protestants. There were Catholics, Eastern Orthodox Christians, and Jews. Not only that, but the public schools were in part established in order to Americanize those immigrant and non-Protestant children. And lowest-common-denominator Protestantism was a vital part of that Americanization.

Catholics Among the Protestants

As it was in the Colonial era, Catholics were suspect. Years of polemics beginning at the Reformation convinced most Protestants that Catholicism wasn't even Christianity. Instead the Church of Rome was "the Whore of Babylon" ruled by the "the popish Anti-Christ." One prominent minister, Lyman Beecher, warned in his extremely popular 1837 book *Plea for the West* that the pope, the Austrian emperor, and assorted European kings, after conspiring together, were sending Catholic immigrants to the United States as agents of sedition and as an army whose aim was to conquer the entire Mississippi Valley. Catholics, after all, had allegiance to a foreign head of state, the pope. As a result, they could not be trusted to be loyal Americans.

Added to this was the 1832 encyclical *Mirari Vos* in which Pope Gregory XVI argued against ideas that were central to the ethos of America in the mid-1800s.[2] He condemned "indifferentism," the notion that theological differences make no difference, but that all sincere, moral, religious people go to Heaven. "Sectarian" ideas make all the difference in the world, and salvation is to be found inside, not outside the Church. He further objected to the belief that liberty of conscience must be maintained for all people at all times. "When all restraints are removed by which men are kept on the narrow path of truth," he wrote, "their nature, which is already inclined to evil, propels them to ruin." Finally, he objected to the belief that the separation of church and state is desirable. That kind of separation leaves the state without its source of morality, resulting in gross immorality and spiritual error to the detriment of the state and her citizens.

Lest we condemn the pope, consider first that his words seem to have been prophetic. We are living his concerns. Second, understand that the primary difference between Pope Gregory's position and the one held by most Protestant Americans at the time was one of transparency. Having the upper hand, the Protestant majority attempted to impose their kind of Christianity on everyone else, but they acted as if there they were obeying the establishment clause and allowing free exercise. That is, the Protestant majority established religion while claiming that they did no such thing.

Hypocrisy? Possibly, but more likely the culture was such that they simply didn't see what they were doing.

In any event, to save the republic from rampant conspiratorial Catholicism (and to keep jobs from poor immigrants who would work for lower wages than native born Americans), the Order of the Star Spangled Banner was formed in 1849. Their core issue was the abolition of slavery (an extremely worthy goal), but they fueled that good cause by adding popular anti-Catholic bigotry to their platform. The Order was a secret society, and when asked about it, members were bound by oath to say, "I know nothing." Hence, they became known as the Know-Nothings. Politically they were called the American Party or the Nativist Party.

Their idea of the First Amendment's establishment clause meant keeping Catholics and Catholicism ("sectarianism") at bay while continuing to strengthen the lowest-common-denominator ("non-sectarian") Protestantism taught in the public schools. When Catholics established their own parochial schools, Know-Nothings and others did their best to see that no public funds went to the "sectarian" schools. The goal was to make it more difficult for poor Catholics to send their children to Catholic schools, forcing them into the public schools with their Protestant bias, teachings, and ethos.

This position was nearly set into concrete in the U. S. Constitution when in 1879 President Ulysses S. Grant proposed an amendment banning "sectarian" religious instruction in public schools and the use of tax dollars to in any way support "sectarian" schools.

The proposed Blaine Amendment, named for James G. Blaine who had been Speaker of the House, read: "No State shall make any law respecting an establishment of religion, or prohibiting the free exercise thereof; and no money raised by taxation in any State for the support of public schools, or derived from any public fund therefor, nor any public lands devoted thereto, shall ever be under the control of any religious sect; nor shall any money so raised or lands so devoted be divided between religious sects or denominations."

Protestants and non-religious people loved the amendment, and while it was never ratified, all but eleven states passed Blaine amendments or similar legislation.

What Grant, Blaine, and the amendment's supporters didn't take into account is that "sectarian" is in the eye of the beholder. When they said sectarian they were talking about Catholics, but "sectarian" came to mean *any* religious based enterprise.

This is perhaps most clearly illustrated by the founding in 1947 of Protestants and Other Americans United for the Separation of Church and State (POAU). Like the Know-Nothings one hundred years earlier, they were concerned with public money in any way benefitting private—that is, Catholic—schools and with Catholic influence in politics. Like the Know Nothings, the organization believed that Catholicism was a great threat to democracy, freedom, and the nation.

Beginning in the 1970s, however, there arose what POAU considered a new threat to democracy, freedom, and the nation: the Christian right. Evangelical Protestants, long on the sidelines politically, suddenly came into the battle with organizations such as Jerry Falwell's Moral Majority and Pat

Robertson's Christian Coalition. In addition, Evangelicals began starting their own schools as non-Catholic alternatives to public education. It had to be stopped.

The "Protestants and Other" part of the name was dropped, and the idea of "sectarian" was extended to Evangelical Protestants. Americans United went from being an anti-Catholic organization to an anti-religious organization despite its president who is a United Church of Christ minister.

The struggle for our religious liberty is as old as the Constitution. We are still trying to find the extent and limits of religious liberty. It is still a live issue in the culture and in the courts. And it's to the history of religious liberty in the courts that we turn now.

2. The Supreme Court and the Great Wall

While everyone knows the phrase "the wall of separation between church and state," most people have no idea where it comes from. Many, in fact, believe it's in the Constitution or perhaps some other important official national document. The wall, we are told must be kept "high and impregnable" lest the state take over the church or—far worse in the minds of many—the church take over the state.

This idea of a "wall of separation" has been used repeatedly over the past decades and is used regularly today to intimidate, silence, or ignore religious voices in the public square. It's the reason public schools have "Winterfest" rather than Christmas. It's the cause of lawsuits against crosses on mountains, Ten Commandments displays in courthouses, prayer circles before high school football games, and crèches outside city halls.

Perhaps worst of all, this wall of separation between church and state is the reason many self-identified Catholic politicians cite for defending abortion on demand, the redefinition of marriage to include same-sex couples, and a host of other dubious ideas. While they claim they are "personally opposed" to such things, the wall, they say, prevents them from advocating their personal opposition in the making of law and public policy.

Without understanding the history of the wall of separation and a few other key ideas, we will never understand the current threats to religious liberty, let alone be in a position to fight for religious liberty properly understood.

Politics as Usual

It all began with the presidential election of 1800. In a rematch of the 1796 presidential election, Thomas Jefferson ran against incumbent president John Adams in what was one of the most divisive campaigns of all time.

Connecticut's established state church was the Congregational Church, and the Connecticut Congregationalists attacked Jefferson viciously in 1800 just as they had in 1796. As far as they were concerned, Jefferson was an atheist and an imminent danger to the republic if not to Western Civilization.

In his book *Thomas Jefferson and the Wall of Separation Between Church and State,* American University professor Daniel Dreisbach notes that in 1798 the influential Congregationalist minister and president of Yale, Timothy Dwight, warned that if Jefferson was elected, "we may see the Bible cast into a bonfire, the vessels of the sacramental supper borne by an ass in public procession, and our children... chanting mockeries against God . . . [to] the ruin of their religion and the loss of their souls."[3]

A politician, like the proverbial elephant, never forgets, and once Jefferson became president, he was still seething at those who implied that if you voted for Jefferson you clearly hated God. On top of that, unlike Presidents Washington and Adams who preceded him, Jefferson believed the First Amendment prevented him as president from making any religious proclamations. As a result he declared no national days of thanksgiving or national days of prayer, which only added fuel to his enemies' fire and brought more charges of atheism and anti-religion.

Of course, not everyone in Connecticut was a Congregationalist and not everyone hated Jefferson. The Baptists, a barely tolerated religious minority in the state, thought Jefferson was wonderful. In fact, they thought that he was so wonderful that the Baptists in Cheshire, Connecticut presented him with a remarkable gift. In 1802 they delivered a 1,235 pound wheel of cheese to the White House. It was, the Baptists declared, "The greatest Cheese in America, for the greatest Man in America." (Yes, this is a true story.)[4]

That same year, the Baptists in Danbury, Connecticut wrote Jefferson a letter asking for help. Religious liberty, they complained, was conspicuously lacking in Congregationalist Connecticut. "[W]hat religious privileges we enjoy (as a minor part of the State,)" they wrote, "we enjoy as favors granted, and not as inalienable rights: and these favors we receive at the expense of such degrading acknowledgements, as are inconsistent with the rights of freemen."[5]

The Baptists had to entreat the state of Connecticut's permission to live their faith. They paid taxes to support Congregational churches and clergy. They paid fines for not attending Congregational churches on Sundays. They could be denied the use of meetinghouses and the ability to perform legally binding weddings. That is, they were tolerated and, as a result, they were not free.

Jefferson knew that his reply to the Danbury Baptists would not be private. It would be published widely and read by everyone. So he carefully drafted and redrafted his reply with three goals in mind: (1) encourage the Baptists, (2) rebuke the Congregationalists who, he felt quite sure, wanted their church to become the national church, and (3) defend his refusal to issue religious proclamations from the White House.

"Religion," he wrote, "is a matter which lies solely between Man & his God." While laws regulating behavior were legitimate, laws regulating belief were not. And that is why "I contemplate with sovereign reverence that act of the whole American people which declared that their legislature should 'make no law respecting an establishment of religion, or prohibiting the free exercise thereof,' thus building a wall of separation between Church & State."[6]

That's right, the metaphorical "wall of separation" comes not from an official document, but from Jefferson's extremely political letter to a group of supporters. There is not and never was anything official about it.

Though Jefferson wrote to reassure the Danbury Baptists, his metaphor of a wall startled them. Walls, after all, have two sides. A wall keeps me out of your yard and you out of mine. And while the Baptists were happy to keep the state out of church business, they feared that this wall would be used to push all religious influences out of public life. With the vehemently secular and anti-religious Hell that was the French Revolution still fresh in everyone's minds, the idea was terrifying.

Jefferson, however, had no intentions of kicking churches or Christians out of the affairs of the state. While no friend of Christianity or any Christian church, he attended the Sunday services that were held in the Capitol Building at government expense. He supported religious observances at the University of Virginia, a state school. And he appropriated (with reservations) federal money for Christian missionaries to Native Americans. All of these actions would cause modern day "wall of separation" advocates to knock each other over in the rush to file lawsuits. Jefferson, however, believed these were consistent with the First Amendment and with his metaphor of a wall.

Having said that, there is no question that, in his letter to the Danbury Baptists, Jefferson reinterpreted the First Amendment. He took the emphasis off the non-establishment of religion and injected the idea of separation. In that, however, he did not advocate the sort of anti-religious bias we see today in so much of church/state jurisprudence. That, as we'll see, came later.

Mormons and Marriage

For more than seventy years no one seems to have thought much about the letter to the Danbury Baptists or Jefferson's metaphoric wall of separation between church and state. Then Joseph Smith began having visions and founded the

Church of Jesus Christ of Latter Day Saints. One tenet of Smith's new religion was a revival of polygamy, one of the practices that resulted in the Mormon pilgrimage west to the U. S. Territory of Utah were they settled in 1847.

Polygamy was illegal in the United States and in all her territories. Since the Mormons practiced polygamy in a U. S. territory, it was just a matter of time before there was a conflict and a major court case.

That case (*Reynolds v. United States*) came in 1874 when George Reynolds, Mormon leader Brigham Young's secretary, married a second wife and became the Mormons' test case challenging anti-polygamy law. If, as a Mormon, Reynolds had a religious duty to marry multiple wives, wasn't he protected by the First Amendment's free exercise clause?

The case was decided by the Supreme Court in 1878 and in 1878, there was no chance in the world that the Court was going to redefine marriage (something I wish we could say about the Court today).

While Reynolds lost, the Supreme Court's opinion affirmed the First Amendment and the right to free exercise of religion! Calling polygamy "odious," the Court opined, "Laws are made for the government of actions, and while they cannot interfere with mere religious belief and opinions, they may with practices."[7]

Note the phrase "mere religious belief and opinions." While most of America was vehemently Protestant, we can already see hints that religious knowledge was being dismissed as second tier knowledge. "Practices," that is, hard facts, had already begun to claim status as preeminent knowledge—the only knowledge worthy of the name and the *real* stuff of life. "Mere" was a harbinger of bad things to come—bad things that have come.

Mormons, the Court concluded, have the right to believe anything they please including the "odious" notion that polygamy is the will of God. Congress may make no law governing religious beliefs. But just as those who believe in the necessity of human sacrifice may not kill people and those who believe widows should be burned on their husbands' funeral pyres may not burn widows (the two examples the Court cited), Mormons have no right to act on their belief in polygamy by actually marrying more than one wife. "To permit this," they wrote, "would be to make the professed doctrines of religious belief superior to the law of the land, and in effect to permit every citizen to become a law unto himself. Government could exist only in name under such circumstances."[8]

Citing Jefferson's letter to the Danbury Baptists, the Court concluded that its ruling was just what the founders had in mind when they protected free exercise. Granting Jefferson a measure of infallibility, they wrote, "Coming as this does from an acknowledged leader of the advocates of the measure, it may be accepted almost as an authoritative declaration of the scope and effect of the amendment thus secured. Congress was deprived of all legislative power over mere opinion [there's that word "mere" again], but was left free to reach actions which were in violation of social duties or subversive of good order."

On the one hand, outlawing polygamy is, I believe, a good thing. Would that our current Supreme Court defended marriage between one man and one woman as vigorously. On the other hand, as Kevin Seamus Hasson notes, "Some right. You can think all you want, you just can't act on your thoughts. If this doesn't sound terribly free (or, for that matter, much like exercise) anymore, that's because it's not."

After the Reynolds case the letter to the Danbury Baptists with its the wall of separation slipped back into obscurity. Seventy years later, it reemerged as an entirely new beast.

From Metaphor to Monster

In the 1940s school busses took students to public schools while city busses took students to private and parochial schools. Since education was important, the state of New Jersey (and others) reimbursed the city bus fare paid by private and parochial school students, 96% of whom attended Catholic schools.

A New Jersey taxpayer, Arch Everson, complained that this was unconstitutional. The reimbursements handed over public monies to private organizations and "forced inhabitants to pay taxes to help support and maintain schools which are dedicated to, and which regularly teach, the Catholic Faith." This, he argued, was a violation of the First Amendment since reimbursing bus fare indirectly aided religion and thus violated the Establishment Clause.

When the Supreme Court decided *Everson v. Board of Education*, it sided against Everson. The Court sidestepped the First Amendment question and ruled it constitutional to allocate taxpayers' money for private uses even in the case of bus fares that were used to take students to religious schools. Religious liberty was safe—sort of.

The "sort of" is there because the Court felt it needed to "clarify" the First Amendment and did so in unhelpful ways. "The 'establishment of religion' clause of the First

Amendment," they wrote, "means at least this: Neither a state nor the Federal Government can set up a church."

Wait a minute, you say. The First Amendment was a compromise specifying that *the Federal Government* cannot set up a church, but allowing the states to do so. What happened?

Answer: the Fourteenth Amendment. The amendment passed in 1868 in the wake of the Civil War in order to protect freed slaves who were now citizens. The amendment has been construed in such a way that the Bill of Rights including the Establishment Clause governs the actions of all states, territories, and municipalities as well as Congress.

The Court in *Everson* insisted further that the Establishment Clause means that neither federal nor state laws can help any or all religions, "force or influence" anyone to attend or not attend church, force or influence anyone to believe or not believe any doctrine, or levy taxes that would support religion even indirectly. Summing up the ruling, they wrote, "Neither the state nor the Federal Government can openly or secretly, participate in the affairs of any religious organizations or groups and vice versa."

The government should certainly stay out of church affairs, but that "vice versa" is troubling. Yet it could not be otherwise because in *Everson* the Court interpreted the First Amendment as erecting "a wall between church and state," adding, "That wall must be kept high and impregnable. We could not approve the slightest breach."

While they didn't believe that New Jersey reimbursing transportation to Catholic school children constituted a breach of this "high and impregnable" wall, the opinion is a long, long way from what Jefferson, Madison, and the other founders had in mind. The Danbury Baptists' fears were taking shape in reality.

Subsequent Supreme Court cases (not counting state court cases) continued this disturbing trend and unraveled the lowest-common-denominator Protestantism that reigned in the schools.

Voluntary religious instruction in public schools was ruled unconstitutional in 1948 (*McCollum v. Board of Education*). The decision stated that "the First Amendment rests upon the premise that both religion and government can best work to achieve their lofty aims if each is left free from the other within its respective sphere." That is, when each stays on its own side of the "high and impregnable" wall.

From there, school prayer was banned piecemeal beginning in 1962 with *Engel v. Vitale*. In this case, a Jewish family complained about the voluntary, state-written, and on the surface uncontroversial prayer for the beginning of the school day: "Almighty God, we acknowledge our dependence upon Thee, and we beg Thy blessings upon us, our parents, our teachers and our Country." In spite of the voluntary and rather mundane nature of the prayer, the Supreme Court ruled the prayer "a practice wholly inconsistent with the Establishment Clause."

The American people as a whole were religiously Protestant and did not take kindly to the ruling. As protests against the *Engel* ruling mounted, the Court felt it needed to clarify and settle the question of religion in public schools. They thought they could do that in 1963 in *Abington School District v. Schempp*, the case against school prayer that included the complaint lodged by Madalyne Murray O'Hair, the vocal founder of American Atheists.

Edward Schempp, a Unitarian Universalist, and O'Hair, the atheist, complained that starting the school day with a reading from the King James Bible (Psalm 23 in the classrooms I was in) and the recitation of the Lord's Prayer constituted the establishment of religion. The Court agreed and school prayer vanished even as the controversies over prayer in school grew. The Court clarified nothing.

In his dissent, Justice Potter Stewart spoke for many if not in 1963, certainly today. He wrote, "If religious exercises are held to be an impermissible activity in schools, religion is placed in an artificial and state-created disadvantage. . . . And a refusal to permit religious exercises thus is seen, not as the realization of state neutrality, but rather as the establishment of a religion of secularism, or at least, as governmental support of the beliefs of those who think that religious exercises should be conducted only in private."

Despite Justice Stewart's wise words, over time the Court also ruled that adult-led prayers at graduation ceremonies and student-led prayers before football games were also violations of the Establishment Clause and had to stop.

Getting beyond school prayer, in November 2013, the Supreme Court heard oral arguments in the case of *Greece v. Galloway*. The town council of Greece, New York had for years begun its meetings with a prayer offered by one of the town's religious leaders. These included Christians, Jews, Baha'is, and even Wiccans though, given the town's demographics, Christians predominate. Does this mean Greece is in violation of the Establishment Clause? Jefferson and

Madison would answer with a resounding "No!" It is perhaps a sign of good tidings to come that on May 5, 2014,
the Court by a vote of five to four also answered, "No." "The
town of Greece," wrote Justice Kennedy in the majority opinion, "does not violate the First Ammendment by opening its
meetings with prayer that comports with our tradition and
does not coerce participation by nonadherents."[9]

Will this clear the muddy waters? Not completely, but it
will certainly help.

Religion as "Toxic Waste"

Beginning with *Everson*, courts began to treat religion as,
to use the phrase of Jordan Lorance of Alliance Defending
Freedom, "toxic waste."[10] Religion is radioactive and poison,
a danger that must be kept behind a "high and impregnable"
wall lest it offend, coerce, influence, infect or, worst of all,
convince some innocent bystander.

This kind of "wall," as some have argued, is really a prison
wall intended to allow the state to manage and control religion while keeping it out of the public square—the polar
opposite of what the founders intended. Others have called
this new and improved "high and impregnable" wall a "spite
fence" illustrating the government's distrust, hatred, and
enmity toward religion and religious bodies.

Daniel Dreisbach cites the late Chief Justice William
Rehnquist who said in 1985, the "'wall of separation between
church and State' is a metaphor based on bad history, a
metaphor which has proven useless as a guide to judging. It
should be frankly and explicitly abandoned."[11] In short, the
metaphor became a monster and the monster is loose today.

Our hope is that the Supreme Court, knowing that church/state jurisprudence is a tangle of strange and even contradictory rulings, will use current and future cases (perhaps beginning with *Greece v. Galloway*) to address the mess in ways that will restore our eroding religious liberty.

CHAPTER FOUR

Storm Clouds Gathering

WE live in an era in which the hostility toward religion has never been greater. Secularizing influences shaped American culture in profound ways. Darwinism, Marxism, radically skeptical biblical scholarship, and a sexual ethos that runs contrary to Christian belief took the country by storm. Slowly at first, but with increasing rapidity, culture changed to accommodate these ideas. And today many Americans are no longer seeking freedom *of* religion, but freedom *from* religion. The battlegrounds include marriage, family, sexuality, contraception, abortion, euthanasia, healthcare, employment law, education, and property law. Increasingly religious liberty is under attack by government, the courts, the media, colleges and universities, and interest groups for whom orthodox Christianity is an obstacle.

This chapter could have two effects. First, it could make you angry. Even this small sample of the many injustices against religious people is more than enough to infuriate.

Anger, however, will not sustain long-term action. And while there is "righteous anger," for most of us the "righteous" part burns off quickly and we're left with all-too-human and all-too-sinful fury. We either stay furious, thereby becoming insufferable and useless, or our anger cools into bitterness. Either way, it doesn't help. We need prayerfully to control our anger.

The second effect could be resignation leading to despair. After all, if it's really as bad as all that and if it may well get even worse, what is the point of fighting? Better to just hunker down, keeping your head low and your mouth shut.

My hope is that in recounting the trouble all around us, rather than becoming angry, we'll grow in compassion for the enemies of religious liberty. They are at best deeply confused and at worst without God in this world and without hope in the next. Jesus told us, "You have heard that it was said, 'You shall love your neighbor and hate your enemy.' But I say to you, love your enemies, and pray for those who persecute you, that you may be children of your heavenly Father, for he makes his sun rise on the bad and the good, and causes rain to fall on the just and the unjust" (Matthew 4:43-45).

Second, rather than resignation and despair, I pray we will grow in our resolve to stand up for the Gospel and for all that is good, true, and beautiful. The last two chapters have made it clear that religious liberty has never been perfectly implemented. It ebbs and flows. Rights denied can be restored if not in this generation, then in some later generation. As so many of the saints of old knew, opposition, no matter how overwhelming, is no excuse to avoid doing the right thing.

With that in mind, let's look at examples of the present threats to religious liberty from government, the courts, colleges and universities, and in the military.

Government and the Management Religion

The threat government poses to religious liberty in the United States is hardly new. While the examples in this section are from the Obama Administration, the desire to scuttle religious liberty and replace it with state directed "freedom of worship" or "religious toleration" was with us during the Clinton administration as well.

John Shattuck served as Assistant Secretary of State for Democracy, Human Rights, and Labor under President Clinton. In that post, he was charged with promoting and protecting human rights including religious liberty throughout the world.

But speaking at a 2002 human rights conference at Harvard University, Shattuck said "Freedom of religion is predicated upon the existence of more than one religion. But a multiplicity of religions has always meant conflict, and religious conflict often led to war and human devastation. This was the state of reality for centuries and millennia, and it is hardly a ringing endorsement of religious freedom."[1]

Rather than religious freedom, Shattuck suggested we substitute religious toleration, which, as we have already seen, is a creation of the state rather than an inalienable human right. As William Saunders of Americans United for Life noted, Shattuck "and the philosophical liberalism he represents, sees religion, unlike other human rights, as a problem, as a source of conflict, as something to be managed."[2]

It is precisely this desire to manage religion, religious ideas, religious organizations, and religious believers that we have seen since President Obama's inauguration in January 2009.

Even as a candidate Barack Obama eschewed the phrase "religious freedom," but with his speech about the November 5, 2009 shootings at Fort Hood, President Obama and then Secretary of State Hillary Clinton began freely substituting the phrase "freedom of worship" for "freedom of religion." Freedom of worship is usually understood as the right to private belief and practice of faith at home and in designated places of worship. It excludes the rights associated with freedom of religion such as evangelism, conversion, raising children in the faith, training and appointing spiritual leaders, and advocating in the public square public morality and policies that are consistent with faith.

Despite the administration's protestations that they are using "freedom of religion" and "freedom of worship" interchangeably in order to be sensitive to Muslims, President Obama's domestic and foreign policies show a marked tilt away from freedom of religion to the watered-down freedom of worship.

What else could explain the administration's arguments in the Supreme Court case *Hosanna-Tabor v. Equal Employment Opportunities Commission (EEOC)*?

The Bid to Control the Ministry

At the center of *Hosanna-Tabor v. EEOC* was the question of "ministerial exceptions." Religious organizations—in this case a Lutheran school—have the right to hire and fire employees based on their internal religious criteria. That is, while it is against the law for Apple or Home Depot to discriminate based on an employee's religion, it is legal for Hosanna-Tabor Lutheran School or St. Bartholomew's Catholic Church to do so.

This means in practice that if a Lutheran congregation is hiring a new director of Christian education and a highly qualified Baptist applies, the congregation may rule him or her out simply because he or she is not Lutheran. And, of course, it also means that a Baptist congregation may legally reject Lutheran, Catholic, Jewish, atheist, or any other non-Baptist applicants.

How, you ask, could it be otherwise? Catholic parishes and schools should have Catholic teachers and Lutheran congregations and schools should have Lutheran teachers. It makes perfect sense.

Yet the Obama Administration argued just the opposite.

The Hosanna-Tabor School in Redford, Michigan dismissed one of its teachers for doctrinal reasons since, in addition to teaching normal school subjects, she also taught religion, led students in prayer, and served as a model of Christian living. She sued claiming discrimination.

The Obama Justice Department argued on her behalf that there should be no legitimate ministerial exemption and that even a priest, minister, or rabbi has the right to sue over religious discrimination based on government regulations. That is, they argued that government employment rules trump the religious liberty of churches, church schools, and other religious organizations.

In a stinging defeat for the Obama Administration and a stunning victory for religious liberty, the U. S. Supreme Court decided the case in favor of Hosanna-Tabor and the ministerial exemption by a vote of 9-0, calling the administration's position "extreme" and "untenable." In the decision, Chief Justice Roberts wrote, "We cannot except the remarkable view that the Religious Clauses [in the First Amendment] have nothing to say about a religious organization's freedom to select its own ministers."

Stinging defeat or not, the administration seems bent on doing everything in its power to force religious believers into conformity with government values, rules, and expectations.

Healthcare and Religious Liberty

In 2007, Belmont Abbey College, a Catholic school in North Carolina, discovered that its health insurance plan covered abortion, contraception, and voluntary sterilization. In response, the college brought the plan into conformity with Catholic Church teachings and eliminated those services from the plan. Eight faculty members filed complaints with the EEOC. The EEOC concluded in March 2009 that there was no evidence of discrimination.[3] Belmont Abbey is, after all, a Catholic college and everyone working there knows it.

Then on July 30, 2009, once the Obama Administration had filled key appointments at EEOC, that decision was reversed and Belmont Abbey was charged with gender discrimination.[4] To put it more starkly, Belmont Abbey's religious and moral beliefs were ruled discriminatory because they were out of line with the prevailing culture and the "reproductive rights" goals of the administration. While the EEOC took no action against Belmont Abbey, the reversal was a harbinger of things to come as a result of the Affordable Care Act (ACA), known popularly as Obamacare.

On March 23, 2010, President Obama signed the ACA into law after it passed the House and Senate. In order to secure the votes necessary for passage, President Obama assured prolife members of Congress that he would sign an executive order to "ensure that Federal funds are not used for abortion services."[5]

Nonetheless, once a bill becomes a law, the administration writes regulations stating how that law will be enforced. In the case of ACA, they spell out the details of what the required health insurance plans will and will not cover.

In February 2011, the Department of Health and Human Services (HHS) issued ACA regulations that require all employee health insurance plans to cover—at no charge to the employee—contraceptives, abortion-inducing drugs, and sterilization. This is the so-called "HHS mandate."

The media has tirelessly referred to it as the "contraception mandate" in an attempt to make it an issue of Catholics against all the sane and right-thinking people in the world. But "contraception mandate" is a misnomer. The mandate demands that all health insurance programs include not just free contraceptives, but also free abortion-inducing drugs and free sterilizations, things that are morally abhorrent to more than just Catholics.

Such regulations typically contain exceptions for those who have religious or other conscience objections and these regulations are no exception. There is a religious conscience exemption, but the exemption is unconscionably narrow. Churches and entities such as schools attached to churches are exempt. But religious hospitals, religious colleges and universities, religious charities, and other religious organizations are not exempt. They must provide insurance that includes free contraceptives, abortion-inducing drugs, and sterilization.

The regulations also lack conscience protection for for-profit businesses owned by people of faith who do not wish to pay for services they believe to be contrary to the teaching of their religion and thus immoral.

After religious groups raised objections, the administration offered "accommodations" that were little more than accounting sleight of hand that changed nothing.

On June 28, 2013 when the regulations became final, Congressman Jeff Fortenberry (R-NE) remarked, "The fundamental problem here is that the government has no business deciding who is religious enough to qualify for their exemption. . . . This is a matter of deeply-held principle, the right of conscience, and religious freedom. The government should be upholding these essential rights, not coercing people to act against them."[6]

The result of the administration's refusal to honor religious freedom has, as we would expect, resulted in lawsuits. These have brought together Catholic schools such as Belmont Abbey and Thomas Aquinas College with Evangelical schools such as Wheaton College and Colorado Christian College, Evangelically owned companies such as Hobby Lobby with Mennonite owned Conestoga Wood Specialties Corporation, Catholic organizations such as EWTN with Evangelical organizations such as Reaching Souls International.

In "Standing Together for Religious Freedom: An Open Letter to All Americans," a large and broad ecumenical group of signatories led by Archbishop William Lori, Chairman of the United States Conference of Catholic Bishops Ad Hoc

Committee for Religious Liberty and Southern Baptist theologian Russell Moore, President of the Ethics & Religious Liberty Commission, affirmed:

> Through its contraceptive coverage mandate, the U.S. Department of Health & Human Services (HHS) continues to breach universal principles affirmed and protected by the U.S. Constitution and other federal laws. While the mandate is a specific offense, it represents a greater fundamental breach of conscience by the federal government. Very simply, HHS is forcing Citizen A, against his or her moral convictions, to purchase a product for Citizen B. The HHS policy is coercive and puts the administration in the position of defining—or casting aside—religious doctrine. This should trouble every American.[7]

The U. S. Supreme Court has taken up the for-profit cases first and on June 30, 2014, the U. S. Supreme Court announced its decision in *Burwell v. Hobby Lobby Stores, Inc.*, a case that includes Conestoga Wood Products and Mardel. The 5–4 decision found in favor of Hobby Lobby and the others against the demands of the Department of Health and Human Services (HHS) that administers the Affordable Care Act.

In the case, the government argued that the HHS mandate applies to the corporations and not to the individuals who own the corporations. The owners may have religious liberty, but their corporations have none. Thus the owners' religious liberty is left intact despite the fact that they, through their corporations, are forced to pay for products and services they sincerely believe to be immoral.

Justice Alito writing for the majority said to the contrary: "Protecting the free-exercise rights of closely held corporations thus protects the religious liberty of the humans who own and control them" and that "HHS's contraceptive mandate substantially burdens the exercise of religion." Thus Hobby Lobby and similar closely-held businesses will not have to provide all the contraceptives and abortifacients listed in the mandate.

Perhaps most importantly, as Thomas Aquinas College President Michael McLean noted, the majority decision "chastised the government for 'arrogating the authority to provide a binding national answer to this religious and philosophical question,' saying that 'HHS and the principal dissent in effect tell the plaintiffs that their beliefs are flawed,' a step which, 'for good reason, we have repeatedly refused to take.'"

Does this case signal a final victory for religious liberty? Not at all. The Court's majority emphasized that this is a narrow ruling. It has to do with the HHS mandate and corporations owned by small groups of people, in these cases, families. They also made it clear that they were not deciding the cases involving nonprofits, other corporations and healthcare coverage, or any future case that might be imagined. In *this* case, they said, the administration did not prove there was a compelling government interest for the mandate, or that forcing those with religious objections to pay for contraceptives, abortifacients, and sterilization was "the least restrictive means" to accomplish their goals.

Having said that, however, it is a wonderful victory for religious freedom. For this we (1) should be grateful and (2) should take heart as we continue in prayer and in resisting those who wish to truncate our religious liberty.

Defining Religious Doctrine

The most curious and dangerous actions of the Obama Administration have been the ones in which it has claimed the prerogative "of defining—or casting aside—religious doctrine."[8]

In 2008, the Tenth Circuit Court of Appeals faced a religious liberty case regarding the Church of Cognizance (*U.S. v. Quaintance*). The Church of Cognizance's doctrine included the belief that marijuana is a deity and smoking marijuana is a sacrament. The church leaders, already in prison on drug related charges, claimed that religious liberty properly understood covered their right to their sacrament. The free exercise clause, they said, should set them free and allow them to continue to minister to their adherents by distributing marijuana for religious use.

The court disagreed.

You might have expected that, but the reason the court disagreed goes to the heart of the danger to religious liberty posed by the Obama Administration. The court never questioned whether or not the doctrine about sacramental marijuana was important to the Church of Cognizance. They accepted church teachings on face value and passed no judgment on them. Instead they concluded that the church leaders, "don't sincerely hold the religious beliefs they claim to hold, but instead seek to use the cover of religion to pursue secular drug trafficking activities." That is, the court determined not that the church's marijuana-as-sacrament doctrine was illegitimate, but that the church's leaders didn't really believe the doctrine. They just wanted to smoke and sell dope.

This is a reasonable decision. A judge or any other government official can only do harm by casting him or herself in the role of theologian, attempting to parse out what is or is not important in any given religious system.

And yet increasingly the government has been casting itself in the role of national theologian. Nowhere is that more apparent than in the controversy over the HHS mandate in which the administration seems to believe that religious objections to contraception, abortion, and sterilization are peripheral to faith and thus can and should be ignored.

As Thomas Farr, director of the Religious Freedom Project at the Berkley Center for Religion, Peace and World Affairs, remarked, "What we are seeing here is precisely what the First Amendment was intended to prohibit: state action targeted against the religious consciences of particular religious communities, and intended to attack their conceptions of justice, equality and the common good. It is tyranny, pure and simple. The stakes go beyond the questions of contraception and abortion to the very meaning of American democracy."[9]

As we've seen, the Obama Administration's attempt to revise the relationship between the government and religious believers is not unique to healthcare. It was evident in the administration's arguments in the *Hosanna-Tabor* case and it's evident in the approach the administration and the courts have taken regarding marriage.

Sexuality *Über Alles*

In October 2009, President Obama signed into law "hate crime" legislation. The law added gender, sexual orientation, gender identity, and disability to the classes of people already protected by hate crime laws. While no one will argue that hating others is a good thing, this kind of legislation seeks to control what people believe, that is, it does not define legal and illegal actions, but designates legal and illegal thoughts, beliefs, and feelings.

The same sort of law has been used in other countries, notably Canada, as a means of silencing religious-based speech regarding sexual behavior and sexual orientation. Erik Stanley, senior counsel at the Alliance Defending Freedom, commented, "Bills of this sort are designed to forward a political agenda and silence critics, not combat actual crime. . . . This law is a grave threat to the First Amendment because it provides special penalties based on what people think, feel or believe."[10]

That same month, President Obama nominated Georgetown University law professor Chai Feldblum to the Equal Employment Opportunity Commission. Feldblum is a lesbian and gay activist who, when asked how she would resolve a conflict between sexual liberty and religious liberty responded, "I'm having a hard time coming up with any case in which religious liberty should win."[11] In another context she put it even more bluntly: "Gays win, Christians lose."[12]

Before the Supreme Court struck down key parts of the Defense of Marriage Act (DOMA) in June 2013 thereby allowing same-sex couples to claim federal marriage benefits (more about that in a moment), the Obama Department of Justice (DOJ) announced in February 2011 that it would not defend DOMA. In an outrageous disregard for the constitutionally mandated separation of power between the three branches of government, the administration deemed the law, duly passed by Congress and signed by President Clinton, unconstitutional years before the Supreme Court ever got a hold of it.

At the same time the DOJ called for (but did not receive) "heightened scrutiny" for all laws affecting gender and sexual orientation.[13] This would have had the effect of increasing the likelihood that laws like DOMA would be struck down and would likely have invited lawsuits against religious organizations that hold homosexuality to be sinful while receiving tax-exempt status or federal funding.

Chai Feldblum is apparently not the only member of the Obama Administration "having a hard time coming up with any case in which religious liberty should win" over sexual liberty. The implications for our religious liberty are obvious and dire.

Who Can Marry Whom

Marriage and religion have, throughout history, been tightly connected, perhaps nowhere more so than in the Christian Church. We believe that God established marriage between the first man and the first woman biding them to "be fruitful and multiply," (Genesis 1:28) thereby making procreation inseparable from marriage.

In the Old Testament, God describes his covenantal relationship with his people as a marriage. He is the divine husband; his people are his beloved bride. This carries over in the New Testament where the Church is referred to as the bride of Christ (Revelation 21:9) and as the *Catechism of the Catholic Church* states (1617), "The entire Christian life bears the mark of the spousal love of Christ and the Church."

Within the sacrament of marriage, a man and a woman share the vocation of witnessing to the spousal love between Christ and his Church through the beauty of their marriage (Ephesians 6:28–33) and by their fruitfulness in the begetting and rearing of children.

This understanding of marriage as the covenantal union of one man and one woman is under attack and this attack has serious and deleterious implications for our religious liberty.

Elaine Huguenin and her husband, Jonathan, run Elane Photography in Albuquerque, New Mexico. Back in 2006, Elaine was asked to photograph a commitment ceremony for two lesbians. And to be clear, this was only a privately created ceremony. Neither same-sex civil unions nor same-sex marriages were legal in New Mexico at the time.

Huguenin turned down the business. She and her husband are Christians and she felt that using her gift of artistic expression to celebrate a same-sex relationship would be a violation of her beliefs and thus of her conscience. The lesbian couple went to another photographer who happily took the job.

Nonetheless, the lesbian couple subsequently registered a complaint with the New Mexico Human Rights Commission accusing the Huguenins of discrimination on the basis of sexual orientation. The commission found the Huguenins guilty and imposed a fine. Their appeal led all the way to the New Mexico Supreme Court, which also found the Huguenins guilty of sexual discrimination. The U.S. Supreme

Court declined to hear the Elane Photography case in April 2014.

It is important to note the ideas about religion and religious liberty that accompanied the decision. Writing in agreement with the majority decision, Justice Richard C. Bosson issued a concurrence in which he said that the Huguenins "now are compelled by law to compromise the very religious beliefs that inspire their lives." This, he defended as fundamentally good and necessary adding that "it is the price of citizenship."

If this sounds to you as if the First Amendment protection for the free exercise of religion has been turned upside-down, you've been paying attention. This is tyranny.

Sacrificing religious liberty was the price of citizenship paid in Europe with its state churches, by people who fled to the religious freedom guaranteed in the U. S. Constitution. As Jim Campbell, an attorney with Alliance Defending Freedom, the legal nonprofit that represented the Huguenins told *National Review*, "The idea that free people can be compelled by law to compromise the very religious beliefs that inspire their lives as the price of citizenship is a chilling and unprecedented attack on freedom."[14]

And Elane Photography is not a lone target in this kind of assault on religious freedom. A florist in Washington, inn operators in Vermont, Illinois, and Hawaii, bakers in Colorado, Iowa, and Oregon, and Methodists in New Jersey have all been sued by same-sex couples—who found other vendors that were more than happy to have their business—for declining to lend their talents, property, and tacit approval to same-sex weddings or commitment ceremonies.

In December 2013, an administrative judge issued an order to Jack Phillips owner of Masterpiece Cakeshop in Lakewood, Colorado. Phillips had refused to make a wedding cake for a same-sex couple. The judge told him that he had no choice. Comparing religious objections to marriages for same-sex couples to objections to biracial marriages, he ruled that Phillips better bake wedding cakes for same-sex couples or risk jail time for breaking the state's nondiscrimination laws.

The Colorado Civil Rights Commission in May 2014 agreed, ruling that if Phillips makes any wedding cakes he must make wedding cakes for same-sex couples, regardless of his deeply and sincerely held religious convictions about the meaning of marriage and regardless of the fact that, in Colorado, same-sex couples can't get married with or without his cake. So while Phillips still makes other sorts of cakes for anyone and everyone, he has announced that he's made his last wedding cake awaiting further appeal.

Yet, as Phillips' attorney Nicole Martin told the press, "Every citizen has the right to live and work according to their religious beliefs even if those beliefs are contrary to prevailing liberal orthodoxy of the day." Then she added, "If the government can tell Jack what to think and say, that is a government we should fear."

She's right. We should fear and expect more—much more—of the same across the country.

Religion or Animus?

While there were gaps in religious liberty in the past, religion was nonetheless taken with utmost seriousness. This is no longer the case in our courts, legislatures, colleges, or military. Religion, rather than being taken seriously, is dismissed as meaningless, dangerous, or even evil.

In 1992, the state of Colorado passed a constitutional amendment stating that sexual orientation would not be treated in the same way as race or gender (gender in the old sense of male or female). The amendment declared the state would make no laws, regulations, or policies "whereby homosexual, lesbian or bisexual orientation, conduct, practices or relationships shall constitute or otherwise be the basis of or entitle any person or class of persons to have or claim any minority status, quota preferences, protected status or claim of discrimination."

Gays, lesbians, and bisexuals would be treated like everyone else in Colorado. They would receive no discriminatory special treatment. This was too much for gay rights activists to bear and they sued. The U. S. Supreme Court heard the case (*Romer v. Evans*) and in 1996 struck down the amendment by a vote of six to three.

Defending the amendment, the State of Colorado argued that it had an interest in upholding the rights of *all* its citizens. Those rights included freedom of association and religious freedom. Landlords, employers, vendors, and others who might have religious or personal objections to homosexuality should not be penalized because the state gives homosexuals special status in the law.

My purpose here is not to debate the merits of the amendment, but to highlight the anti-religious bias that struck it down. Writing for the majority, Justice Anthony Kennedy said, "the amendment seems inexplicable by anything but animus toward the class that it affects."

Constitutional law scholar Hadley Arkes writing about *Romer* remains shocked that, "Generations of reflection [about homosexuality], running back to the ancients, could be dismissed as one long, thoughtless spasm of irrational 'animus.'"[15]

But how convenient to attribute every objection to homosexuality and opening up marriage to same-sex couples to "animus." It saves all the time and energy that would otherwise have to be invested in reading, understanding, and responding to the arguments for traditional ideas about sexuality and marriage. Call people "haters" and there's no need to listen to what they say.

Once the Supreme Court decided *Romer* based on alleged animus, the same thinking proliferated in other court cases including the decisions about California's Proposition 8.

Proposition 8 was an amendment to the California constitution. The amendment read, "Only marriage between a man and a woman is valid or recognized in California." The amendment passed handily and then all the trouble started.

Not only was there a lawsuit, but there was reprisal against anyone who supported the measure. The names and addresses of people who contributed to the campaign for Proposition 8 were posted online in order to embarrass, punish, and intimidate. Homosexual activists laid siege to a restaurant in Los Angeles retaliating against the restaurant owner's daughter for contributing $100 to uphold marriage.

Churches supportive of Proposition 8 were vandalized. For example, someone poured adhesive on the doormat, keypad lock, and windows of a Mormon church. Elsewhere eggs and toilet paper were thrown at an Assemblies of God

Church. And a Catholic church in San Francisco—a parish that had *opposed* Proposition 8—was nonetheless spray painted with swastikas and anti-Catholic graffiti.

When the lawsuit against Proposition 8 came to federal court, Judge Vaughn Walker (who later revealed that he was gay) wrote in his opinion striking down the amendment, "Religious beliefs that gay and lesbian relationships are sinful or inferior to heterosexual relationships harm gays and lesbians." And when that happens, to quote Chai Feldblum once again, "Gays win, Christians lose." In this case the people of California also lost.

A final example in this chain of decisions based on alleged animus is the Supreme Court case that struck down most of the Defense of Marriage Act (DOMA) (*U.S. v. Windsor*). DOMA, passed in 1996 and signed into law by President Bill Clinton, said that for federal purposes "marriage" would mean only "a legal union between one man and one woman as husband and wife."

Again, we can debate the merits of DOMA—and if we did, that would be more than what the majority of the justices seem to have done. Rather than considering the arguments offered for the goodness of one-man-one-woman marriage, the majority opinion authored by Justice Kennedy claimed that even the name of the law ("Defense of Marriage Act") was a malicious attack on same-sex couples since it implied that marriage need to be defended against them. The purpose of the law, the decision said, was to "disparage and to injure," "demean," "impose inequity," "impose a stigma," deny "equal dignity," to same-sex couples, and to humiliate their children.

Arguments about how permitting same-sex couples to marry would further weaken marriage and family, how it would harm children by purposely denying them a mom and a dad, and how it opens the door to polygamy, polyamory, and other redefinitions of marriage fell on deaf ears. Animus toward those with same-sex attraction—much of it driven by religion—is the enemy or, as Justice Antonin Scalia put it in his dissent, "the Court's conclusion that only those with hateful hearts could have voted 'aye' on this Act."

Justice Scalia went on: "It is one thing for a society to elect change; it is another for a court of law to impose change by adjudging those who oppose it *hostes humani generis*, enemies of the human race." Yet that same claim of hating humanity made against Christians in the Roman Empire seems to be resurfacing in rulings like *Windsor* and the other cases we've discussed.

School Daze

The story is at once shocking and monotonous.

According to their Facebook page, "See You at the Pole is a student-led, student-initiated movement of prayer that revolves around students praying together on the third Wednesday of September, usually before school and usually at the school's flagpole."

The program has been around for years and had already been through the courts. At this point, even the American Civil Liberties Union (ACLU) approves of it provided that it remains student-led and student-initiated.

Leading up to the September 2013 See You at the Pole, a Kansas City middle schooler identified as K. R. was busily student-leading and student-initiating the ecumenical event. The key to her publicity plan was fliers she printed with information about the event and two Bible verses: "For God so loved the world that he gave his only Son, so that everyone who believes in him might not perish but might have eternal life" (John 3:16) and "But God proves his love for us in that while we were still sinners Christ died for us" (Romans 5:8).

K. R. posted the fliers in appropriate places around the school and handed them out to her classmates.

Then while she was chatting with friends at a school dance, one of the school counselors confronted her. Her manner was forceful and insistent—and, I suspect, inappropriate and embarrassing at a school dance. She told K. R. that her fliers were "illegal" since they violated the separation of church and state. K. R. was ordered to stop distributing her fliers and the ones she had posted were torn down and thrown away.[16]

According to a report on the incident, "other posters at the school were not censored, such as those that promoted school dances, and a poster of rapper Lil' Wayne that read 'Good kush and alcohol' was not disturbed."[17] That is, dances, kush (marijuana), and alcohol were okay to promote in middle school, but information about a student-led and student-initiated prayer gathering had to be censored.

As I said, it's both shocking and monotonous. The lawsuit initiated against the school on K. R.'s behalf by the Alliance Defending Freedom (ADF) was settled with the school backing down. But soon there will be another case to take its place as school administrators continue to misinterpret the law on religious activities in public schools, overreact by erecting their own wall of separation of church and school, and over-reach their authority by denying students their constitutional rights. I will not pass judgment as to whether this happens out of ignorance of the law or hostility toward religion, though I suspect there's a mix in most places.

College Daze

This ignorance and/or hostility is not limited to our public schools. Religious freedom is becoming a scarce commodity on some of our public and private university campuses as well.

On the public side, Christian Legal Society (CLS) has student-led groups in most U.S. law schools. According to the organization's website, "CLS is a membership organization of Christian attorneys, judges, paralegals, law students, and other legal professionals dedicated to serving Jesus Christ through the practice of law, defense of religious freedom, and provision of legal aid to the needy."

CLS meetings are open to anyone who wishes to attend, but in order to vote or hold office in a CLS chapter, an individual must sign the organization's statement of faith:

> Trusting in Jesus Christ as my Savior, I believe in: One God, eternally existent in three persons, Father, Son and Holy Spirit. God the Father Almighty, Maker of heaven and earth. The Deity of our Lord, Jesus Christ, God's only Son, conceived of the Holy Spirit, born of the virgin Mary; His vicarious death for our sins through which we receive eternal life; His bodily resurrection and personal return. The presence and

power of the Holy Spirit in the work of regeneration. The Bible as the inspired Word of God.

Officers in CLS chapters are also expected to live according to the Word of God in their professional and personal lives. And insofar as the Bible excludes sex outside of marriage and homosexual behavior, CLS does as well.

The Outlaws, a gay group at the University of California Hastings College of Law in San Francisco objected to the rules governing membership and leadership at CLS. (Never mind that they had exclusionary membership rules as well.)

The school's administration responded by not letting CLS register as an official student group, and insisting that they allow anyone to join, vote, and hold office regardless of belief or lifestyle. The university, they were told, had an "all-comers" policy for all student organizations. No one could be excluded from any student organization since all were in part funded by university funds and all used university owned facilities.[18]

Hastings has about sixty student groups. It has denied registration based on the "all-comers" rule to exactly one. CLS sued believing that the school denied them registration because it disagrees with their beliefs and thus intended to deny their freedom of speech. In the name of "viewpoint neutrality" the school was, they claimed, guilty of viewpoint discrimination directed against Christians.

When challenged by PBS correspondent Tim O'Brien about the rationality and fairness of the "all-comers" policy, Chancellor and Acting Dean of Hastings, Leo Martinez, defended it in absolute terms.

"Would a student chapter of, say, B'nai B'rith, a Jewish Anti-Defamation League, have to admit Muslims?" asked O'Brien.

"The short answer," replied Martinez, "is yes."

" A black group would have to admit white supremacists?"

"It would."

"Even if it means a black student organization is going to have to admit members of the Ku Klux Klan?"

"Yes."[19]

As Greg Baylor, attorney for the CLS chapter said during the same interview, "It makes no sense for a public university to force the Republicans to have a Young Democrat as their leader. It makes no sense for the environmentalists' group to be forced to have a lumberjack who's out there cutting down trees to be the messenger for it. The Constitution is clear about this. It protects the rights of groups to come together to articulate their messages and to choose their messengers."[20]

Most people would agree. People who want to force everyone to play chess should not be empowered to commandeer the Hastings Basketball Club. The "all-comers" policy—which appears to have been invented for the occasion—is utterly irrational.

Unfortunately, the U. S. Supreme Court (*Christian Legal Society v. Martinez*) did not agree. Five of the justices saw the wisdom in the all-comers policy adopted by Hastings and voted against CLS, claiming that their religious freedom, freedom of speech, or freedom of association were still intact.

In his dissent, Justice Samuel Alito correctly observed "the Court arms public educational institutions with a handy weapon for suppressing the speech of unpopular groups—groups to which, as Hastings candidly puts it, these institutions 'do not wish to . . . lend their name[s].'"

The same kind of pretzel logic has been taken up by private universities as well. Vanderbilt, originally a Methodist school, has applied it to its Christian groups in a decision that appears to have come from the highest authorities in the university.

In an email to the Christian Legal Society at Vanderbilt about their group's newly revised constitution, the then Interim Director of the Office of Religious Life noted, "Article III states that, 'All officers of this Chapter must subscribe to the Christian Legal Society Statement of Faith.' Vanderbilt's policies do not allow any student organization to preclude someone from a leadership position based on religious belief. Only performance-based criteria may be used. This section will need to be rewritten reflecting this policy."

While it may be true that Vanderbilt does not have a vendetta against Christians—though Christian groups are the only ones affected by the policies—the complete misunderstanding of religion, religious beliefs, and the purpose and mission of religious groups is deplorable.

Events at Hastings School of Law, Vanderbilt, and other schools are a clear illustration of how religious liberty is the first liberty. Deny religious liberty and all the other liberties collapse into rubbish. Having been denied religious liberty, CLS at Hastings and at Vanderbilt have no rights to free speech and no rights to free association. They are only acceptable to their respective schools if they remain silent about what they believe, tacitly denying the Gospel in word and deed.

Atheists in Foxholes

"There are no atheists in foxholes," goes the old infantry saying. The smell of gunpowder, the sounds of war, and the nearness of death create perspective that soldiers would perhaps not have otherwise. That is why George Washington in 1776 asked for and received authorization from Congress to place a chaplain in every regiment of his army. Commanding officers were "To see that all inferior officers and soldiers pay them a suitable respect and attend carefully upon religious exercises. The blessing and protection of Heaven are at all times necessary but especially so in times of public distress and danger."[21]

Chaplains, who must on the one hand follow the rules and uphold the doctrines of their endorsing denomination or group must also live within the military chain of command. Thus while a Catholic priest serving as a chaplain in the Army is obliged to obey the archbishop of the Archdiocese for the Military Services, he is also obliged to obey his commanding officers—both within the chaplain corps and outside of it. Increasingly this places chaplains in the position where they need to choose to serve God or Caesar (Matthew 22:21). As a result, today the religious liberty and, indeed, the very existence of the chaplains in our military are in danger.

This is first of all the result of sexuality *über alles* playing itself out in the armed forces. With the repeal of Don't-Ask-Don't-Tell (DADT) and now the end of federal DOMA, gays and lesbians can serve openly in the military and claim marriage benefits. Pentagon policies allow gay and lesbian service members all the rights, privileges, and opportunities offered to other soldiers, sailors, and airmen.

Yet the Archdiocese for the Military Services issued a set of rules for Catholic chaplains that begins, "No Catholic priest or deacon may be forced by any authority to witness or bless the union of couples of the same gender. No Catholic priest or deacon can be obliged to assist at a 'Strong Bonds' or other 'Marriage Retreat', if that gathering is also open to couples of the same gender."[22]

That is, the Archdiocese—as well as many Evangelical Protestant denominations—has rules for their chaplains that are, on some level, at odds with new policies and regulations from the Pentagon.

In order to maintain the religious liberty of the chaplains and their ability to minister within their doctrinal and moral beliefs, a religious liberty amendment was added to the National Defense Authorization Act for 2014 in order to control what has been a growing hostility toward religion and religiously conservative chaplains.

President Obama has vigorously opposed the amendment that calls for "Expansion and implementation of protection of rights of conscience of members of the Armed Forces and chaplains of such members." Using amazing language the White House remarked, "The Administration strongly objects to [this section], which would require the Armed Forces to accommodate, except in cases of military necessity, 'actions and speech' reflecting the 'conscience, moral principles, or religious beliefs of the member.'"[23] That is, it would require the Armed Forces to respect the religious liberty of all personnel.

Sadly, this isn't shocking. During President Obama's tenure, the military has become increasingly unfriendly toward Christians.

Skirmishes and Battles

Volunteer members of the Veterans of Foreign Wars had been making themselves available as an honor guard for funerals at Houston National Cemetery for years. In July 2011, the cemetery, run by the Department of Veterans Affairs informed the honor guards that they could no longer make any reference to God and needed to edit him out of their ceremony.

When the veterans informed the Liberty Institute, lawyers there felt it must have been some misunderstanding. But when they contacted the cemetery, they were met with hostility. The good news is that the veterans are back in the honor guard business. The bad news is that it took a lawsuit to force the Department of Veterans Affairs to respect their religious liberty. That same month, the Air Force discontinued a course in ethics taught at Vandenberg Air Force Base in California, "the only installation in the free world where operational intercontinental ballistic missiles and polar-orbiting space satellites are launched."[24] The course, taught by chaplains, was required for all officers connected with nuclear missiles.

The course quoted from and made references to the Bible. It also required readings about just war theory, an idea that originated with St. Augustine of Hippo in the fourth century and was picked up by St. Thomas Aquinas in the thirteenth century. Just war theory has been part of the training for officers in the United States for years, but this course was suddenly in need of thorough review primarily because of its use of Christian materials for reading and discussion.[25]

Not only has Christianity been excluded from some training, it is being attacked in other training. Copies of training materials from the Army Reserves in Pennsylvania show that in a class about extremism, instructors listed Evangelical Christianity and Catholicism along with Al Qaeda, Hamas, the Muslim Brotherhood, the Klu Klux Klan, and other terrorist groups as examples of "religious extremism."[26]

In January 2012, the Army censored a letter written by Timothy Broglio, Archbishop for Military Services, that was to be read by Catholic chaplains from the pulpit at every Mass on January 29. The letter called on Catholics to resist the HHS Mandate in the Affordable Care Act regulations. When he found out about it, the Army Chief of Chaplains directed that the letter not be read from the pulpit as the archbishop directed his priests. Priests were permitted to mention that there was a letter from the archbishop and that copies of the letter—with the Chief of Chaplain's edits—were available after Mass.

A month later, after complaints from the Military Association of Atheists and Freethinkers, the word "God" was removed from the motto of the Air Force Rapid Capabilities Office. The motto, *Opus Dei Cum Pecunia Alienum Efficemus* (Doing God's Work with Other People's Money) though in Latin and thus incomprehensible to nearly everyone who saw it was deemed offensively religious. The new motto reads, "Doing Miracles with Other People's Money," which ignores the fact that only God can do miracles.[27]

The Air Force in particular has been influenced by Air Force veteran and anti-religion crusader Michael Weinstein. Weinstein founded the Military Religious Freedom Foundation in 2004 after his son complained about the distribution of fliers by fellow cadets urging people to see Mel Gibson's movie "The Passion of the Christ" while attending the Air Force Academy.[28]

Weinstein's group advocates a radical separation of church and state. He has the ear of many high-ranking Air Force officers. Why they are listening to him is a bit of a mystery given his utter lack of religious toleration. Weinstein commented about the actions including evangelization performed by those who hold an orthodox biblical understanding of faith and morality, "Let's call these ignoble actions what they are: the senseless and cowardly squallings of human monsters."[29]

Conclusion

Whenever I mentioned that I was working on a book about the threats to our religious liberty, friends responded with something such as, "I guess you're not finding it too hard to locate examples of the threat." I only wish it was hard. It is far too easy to find examples of the threat to our religious liberty. They are popping up everywhere.

The purpose of this chapter is not to be comprehensive. That would take a much, much longer book and require weekly addenda. Instead, the purpose here is an overview of an administration seemingly at war with the religious liberty of its citizens. The threats will, I believe, get worse before they get better.

Nonetheless, despair is not a Christian position. The early nineteenth century Protestant missionary Adoniram Judson had it right when he said, "The future is as bright as the promises of God."[30] So now that we've traced the history of religious liberty and surveyed the current threats, let's turn to ways in which we can make a difference for the good.

CHAPTER FIVE

Reasserting Our Religious Liberty

AS I said earlier, there has never been a golden age of religious liberty in the United States (and, let me add there never will be). Instead, as we've seen there has been a pushing and pulling in the courts and in the culture to understand how expansive religious liberty is and where its limits lie.

That being said, the conclusions at which the courts and culture have arrived are, to put it mildly, unacceptable and becoming increasingly so.

For example, in 2009, a secularist organization sued two Wisconsin high schools. The schools do not have the space to accommodate graduates, families, friends, and others at the yearly commencement exercises. People were cramped, uncomfortable, and, without air conditioning, hot. To solve the problem the school district, by student request, has for years rented a local church that accommodated everyone comfortably and provided air conditioning.

The secular group claims that by exposing people to a religious building in which there are crosses, hymnals, and other religious symbols, the schools are endorsing religion and coercing faith.

This is another example of treating religion as toxic waste. If children get near it, there's no telling what harm could come to them. The only alternative is to erect the highest and most impregnable wall possible around religion and to put a thick dark curtain over all things religious, thus keeping religion and religiously rooted ideas out of not just the public square, but the public eye.

In June 2014, the U. S. Supreme Court refused to hear this case (Elmbrook School District v. Doe). As a result, the ruling by the Seventh U. S. Circuit Court stands and the schools may no longer rent church facilities for their graduations.

In response to the threats to religious liberty, let me suggest a seven-part plan: understand life in our fallen world, understand the dangers of losing religious liberty, get informed, pray, force the question, evangelize, and, if need be, suffer.

Life in a Fallen World

1) Disputed Kingship

At Mass on the last Sunday of the Christian year, Our Lord Jesus Christ, King of the Universe, the Gospel reading came as a surprise to me. I had probably heard it before, but it didn't strike me the way it did this past year. It's the story of the repentant thief on the cross next to Jesus (Luke 23:35-42).

When Jesus was crucified between two thieves, Pontius Pilate ordered a sign hung on the cross over Jesus' head.

It read: "Jesus of Nazareth, the King of the Jews" (John 19:19-21). The rulers of the Jewish people saw Jesus hanging from the cross, read the sign, and sneered at him, "He saved others, let him save himself if he is the chosen one, the Christ of God." They also complained to Pilate insisting that the sign should read, "This man said he was King of the Jews."

The Roman soldiers, their grisly work done, saw Jesus, read the sign over his head, and jeered at him, "If you are King of the Jews, save yourself."

One thief looked over and reviled him, "Are you not the Christ? Save yourself and us." Jesus made no answer to that thief or to the soldiers or to the rulers. He only responded to the second thief who, after rebuking his fellow thief, pleaded, "Jesus, remember me when you come into your kingdom."

American magazines including *Time*, *U.S. News*, and *Newsweek* never seem to tire of the question this Gospel reading presents: "Who is Jesus?" The rulers among the Jews thought he was a fraud. The Roman soldiers thought he was a fool. The unrepentant thief thought he was a disappointment (at least). During his lifetime, some said he was "John the Baptist, others say Elijah, and others Jeremiah or one of the prophets" (Matthew 16:14). Others said he was demonic or insane (John 10:20). Through the centuries people have believed he was a political leader and martyr, a madman, a spirit who only appeared to have a body, a magician, the perpetrator of the world's greatest hoax, and a fictitious figment of the Church's propaganda machine.

The penitent thief stands out as one of the exceptions. Through the eyes of faith, he saw Jesus hanging helplessly on the cross, his body brutalized, bruised, and bleeding, and recognized him as the King of Kings.

We are faced in our era between the first coming of Jesus as a baby in Bethlehem and the second coming of Jesus as the King of Glory with what scholars have called his "disputed kingship." When he comes again, there will be no question in anyone's mind that he is the King. On that day, "that at the name of Jesus every knee should bend, of those in heaven and on earth and under the earth, and every tongue confess that Jesus Christ is Lord, to the glory of God the Father" (Philippians 2:10–11).

In the meantime, magazines, TV shows, scholars, and school children will go on asking, "Who is Jesus?" The infant in the manger, the boy in the Temple, the traveling preacher in Galilee, and the dying man on the cross with the sign over his head don't seem to add up to the portrait of a king.

Until Jesus returns, his kingship will continue to be in dispute and our faith will continue to be in dispute. Only religious liberty allows every one to ask and answer the question "Who is Jesus?"

2) *Libido Dominandi*

In his magisterial work *The City of God*, St. Augustine of Hippo (AD 354-430) contrasted the City of God with the City of Man. Religious liberty plays out at the intersection of the two.

The Church is the City of God on pilgrimage through this age. It is the divine commonwealth ruled by God and governed by the law of love. Augustine writes: "For if we inquire whence it is, God created it; or whence its wisdom, God illumined it; or whence its blessedness, God is its bliss. It has its form by subsisting in Him; its enlightenment by contemplating Him; its joy by abiding in Him. It is; it sees; it loves. In God's eternity is its life; in God's truth is its light; in God's goodness is its joy."[1]

By contrast, the City of Man is the secular order. It is the earthly city ruled by humans for their own gain using their own rules. Above all, says Augustine, it "is itself ruled by the lust of rule."[2] "The lust of rule" is a translation of the Latin *libido dominandi*. As the late Fr. Richard John Neuhaus put it, *libido dominandi* is "the lust for power, advantage, and glory."[3]

This lust for domination doesn't just characterize politics in the City of Man, it characterizes each of us in this fallen world. The *libido dominandi* is in each of us. It urges us to plot and fight to have our own way and force others do as we say. It is the controlling passion of our fallen nature and, thus, of our fallen world.

As it relates to the threats to religious liberty, we all have the desire to force our beliefs on others, to eliminate challenges to the way we think, to make others over in our image. Religious liberty in this fallen world requires constant vigilance and constant repentance.

3) God-Haunted

What Catholic author Flannery O'Conner said about the American South applies to the whole country. "I think it is safe to say," she wrote, "that while the South is hardly Christ-centered, it is most certainly Christ-haunted."[4] And anyone who is not Christ-haunted is most certainly God-haunted.

While humans may dismiss God, morality, truth, life after death, judgment, and that "narrow-minded" religious upbringing they had, our consciences know better. We are God-haunted whether we like it or not.

As St. Paul wrote to the Christians in Rome, "Ever since the creation of the world, his invisible attributes of eternal power and divinity have been able to be understood and perceived in what he has made" (Romans 1:20) God is obvious as are the moral standards of the Natural Law, but instead of honoring God and living moral lives, we humans suppress the truth that we know in order to do as we please.

But truth has a way of reasserting itself. Conscience attacks us and we have no choice but either to acknowledge truth or find new ways to keep it locked in the cellar. While not all assaults on religious liberty arise out of God-hauntedness and the desire to suppress truth, much hatred of religion, of Christianity in general, and of the Catholic Church in particular bubble up out of this fact of life in our fallen world.

For Christians this should inspire compassion, love, and even tenderness toward those who would rob the American people of our religious liberty. Opponents of religious liberty typically don't know Jesus the King. Instead they waste away their time and energy attempting to dominate others and impose their beliefs while they are haunted by an inner voice that keeps telling them that what they apparently hate is in fact the truth.

The Danger of Losing Religious Liberty

Years ago, coal miners would bring canaries with them to work deep in the Earth. As long as the canaries cheerfully sang, the miners knew all was well. A dead canary, however, meant that the air in the mine was going bad. After the canary died, unless they acted fast, the miners would die too.

Religious liberty is the canary in the coal mine of all our freedoms.

As Catholics, we keep the stories and the memory of the martyrs alive. The Church remembers what happened in the past when religious liberty was abridged.

In France, clergy and laity together celebrated the storming of the Bastille in 1789. The Revolution looked like good news for religious liberty. The Declaration of the Rights of Man stated, "No one shall be disturbed for his opinions, even religious, provided their manifestation does not disturb the public order established by law."[5]

This sounded like religious liberty, but, in truth, it placed the Church under the heel of the state since the state reserved the right to define what "disturb the public order established by law" meant.

The French state soon reorganized the Catholic Church inside its borders, asserting absolute control. Bishops and priests were chosen by popular election. Clergy had to swear an oath of allegiance pledging their first loyalty to the state. Those who refused to swear the oath were hunted down, imprisoned, exiled, or killed as enemies of France.

By 1793, "missionary representatives" were sent into the provinces to close churches, prevent priests from ministering, and root out anyone practicing the Christian religion. And beginning with sixteen cloistered nuns guillotined in Paris on July 17, 1794, many of those declared enemies of the state because of their Christian faith suffered martyrdom.

Freedom of worship, a phrase the Obama administration has been substituting for "religious freedom,"[6] was still the law in France, but it meant (and still means) private religious practice with absolutely no public expression of faith. Public life was to be entirely secular, washed clean of all religious influences, with blood if need be.

The regime subsequently cracked down on freedom of speech, freedom of the press, freedom of association, and freedom to dissent. Once religious liberty was breached, those others were easy.

Many think of Mexico as a Catholic country. This is so incorrect that it would be laughable were it not for all the bloodshed. While the population of Mexico was once ninety percent Catholic at the time, the constitution of 1917 stripped Mexicans of their religious liberty. The result? Oppression, violence, and martyrs.

That constitution stipulated that all religious practices were subject to state regulation. And so the state could— and did—confiscate church property and close most of the churches. Religious charities were shut down even though this left the poor, the sick, and the suffering with no one to care for them. Clergy not approved by the state were harassed, sent into exile, or killed.

The state also took control of public and private education, mandating anti-religious secularism. Teachers took an oath affirming atheism, declaring enmity toward the Church and clergy, and promising "I will not permit any of my household to take part in any religious act whatsoever."

Between 1926 and 1929, "The Years of the Martyrs," a multitude of men, women and children, priests, monks and nuns were killed for their faith by mobs, the army, and government firing squads.

Again, the assault on religious liberty sounded the alarm.

I could go on about Eastern Europe under the Nazis and then the Communists, China, Cuba, Vietnam, Spain.

Spain?

Most of us have forgotten about the Spanish Civil War of 1936-1939, assuming we ever knew the story to begin with. The anti-religious bloodshed was so horrific that of the two hundred sixty six twentieth-century martyrs beatified by Pope John Paul II in 1996, two hundred eighteen were Spanish.

In every case, the warning sign of tyranny was the weakening of religious liberty. The first step a secular state takes in order to fulfill its desire to control the population is the bid to control the Church.

We would like to think it can't happen here, but as the previous chapters demonstrate, the canary is, if not dead, extremely ill. It's already happening here. The threat to all our liberties is clear, present, and grave.

Getting in the Loop

When a friend was speaking to a group of Christian businesspeople in a small city, he addressed the threat to our religious liberty. He mentioned the "HHS mandate." No one knew what he was talking about. He addressed the threat to marriage posed by "LGBT" groups. No one knew that he was referring to lesbians, gays, bisexuals, and transgenders. As to the hazard we face regarding religious liberty, the overall attitude of the group was, "It can't happen here."

We will not get the information we need to follow the issue, pray, and take action in our daily newspapers, on cable news, or by reading most news magazines (*World Magazine* being one exception). So where can we go for information about religious liberty?

Below is a list of groups that are fighting to protect our religious freedom along with their web addresses. Most of them in addition to the information on their websites offer email updates. While the groups are not all faith-based, in most cases it's Christian lawyers, policy experts, and activists who are hard at work protecting our freedoms. The list is alphabetical, not in order of priority.

- **Acton Institute** (www.acton.org). Though much of Acton's work focus on economic freedom, they are well aware that without religious freedom, economic freedom is of little value. As a result, their blog, accessible from the website, often features entries about religious liberty.
- **Alliance Defending Freedom** (www.alliancedefend ingfreedom.org) is an alliance of legal professionals who advocate on behalf of those whose liberty is under attack. They have been the lead attorneys in many religious liberty cases including arguing before the U.S. Supreme Court.
- **The American Center for Law and Justice** (www. aclj.org) was founded in 1990 with the mission of protecting religious and constitutional freedoms. Led by Chief Counsel Jay Sekulow, the ACLJ advocates, educates, and litigates to protect freedom and liberty

in the United States and around the world. The ACLJ has argued before the Supreme Court on many occasions and runs one of the most effective amicus brief programs in the country.

- **Americans United for Life** (www.aul.org) is a nonprofit law firm primarily focused on the life issues—abortion, end-of-life, and bioethics. Because of this, their portfolio of issues includes conscience protection for healthcare professionals who have religious and moral objections to participating in abortion or euthanasia.

- **The Becket Fund** (www.becketfund.org) is a nonprofit law firm and educational institute defending religious liberty. According to their website, they exist "to vindicate a simple but frequently neglected principle: that because the religious impulse is natural to human beings, religious expression is natural to human culture."

- **The Catholic Benefits Association** (www.lifeaffirm ingcare.com) was formed in 2014 under the leadership of several Catholic bishops in response to the Affordable Care Act's contraceptive and abortifacient mandate. Through the Catholic Insurance Company which it owns, CBA works to provide both nonprofit and for-profit employers with life-affirming health coverage consistent with Catholic values.

- **The Catholic League** (www.catholicleague.org) describes itself as a "Catholic civil rights organization." They monitor assaults on Catholics and other

Christians made in the media, the press, and the public square.

- **Chaplains Alliance for Religious Liberty** (www. chaplainsalliance.org) focuses its attention entirely on religious liberty in the armed forces, with a special emphasis on the freedom of chaplains to preach the fullness of the Gospel.

- **Christian Legal Society** (www.clsnet.org) is a nondenominational fellowship of Christian lawyers and law students with chapters at many law schools. In addition to fighting for the religious liberty of their law school chapters, their Center for Law & Religious Freedom argues cases and advises Congress on issues related to religious freedom.

- **The Ethics and Public Policy Center's** (www.eppc. org) American Religious Freedom Project works "to inculcate a sound understanding of America's religious freedoms among state and national government officials, the media, the legal and academic communities, and the public." They have been particularly successful in establishing religious freedom caucuses in many state legislatures.

- **Family Research Council** (www.frc.org) covers a broad spectrum of issues related to faith, freedom, and the family including religious liberty. They also have a lobbying arm that permits them to have greater direct influence into politics in Washington.

- *First Things* (www.firstthings.org) is a journal focused on religion and public life. That, of course, includes issues of religious liberty, the right of religious believers to take their most deeply held convictions into the public square.

- **The Heritage Foundation** (www.heritage.org) is a Washington, DC based think-tank whose work includes a division focused on Religion and Civil Society. Their website includes research on particular issues in religious liberty as well as basic materials as to why religious liberty matters to civil society, marriage, family, and the health of the nation.

- **The Hudson Institute** (www.hudson.org) is one of the best sources of information about international religious freedom. Christians are far and away the most persecuted religious group in the world today and the scholars at Hudson's Center for Religious Freedom report on developments worldwide.

- **The Institute on Religion & Democracy** (www.theird.org) has staff dedicated entirely to religious liberty. Their website and blog provide easily accessible information on current domestic and international religious liberty issues.

- **Liberty Counsel** (www.lc.org) is an evangelical group that advocates in court and in the public square for religious liberty, the sanctity of life, and the family. They provide church-based programming, pro-bono legal services, and action alerts.

- **The Manhattan Declaration** (www.manhattandeclaration.org) is a call to all Christians and other people of good will to take a stand for the sanctity of life, the dignity of marriage, and freedom of religion. In addition to being open to additional signatures, the

Manhattan Declaration provides updates concerning life, marriage, and religious liberty.

- **The Religious Freedom Project at Georgetown University** (berkleycenter.georgetown.edu/rfp) "is the nation's only university-based program devoted exclusively to the analysis of religious freedom." This is a scholarly project examining "different understandings of religious liberty as it relates to other fundamental freedoms; its importance for democracy; and its role in social and economic development, international diplomacy, and the struggle against violent religious extremism."

- **The Thomas More Law Center** (www.thomasmore.org) is a non-profit public interest law firm that "defends and promotes America's Judeo-Christian heritage and moral values including the religious freedom of Christians, time-honored family values, and the sanctity of human life.

- **United States Conference of Catholic Bishops** (www.usccb.org). The bishops have been religious liberty heroes over the past years. Their website is stocked with resources to enable Catholics and other Christians to understand what's at stake and what actions we can take to defend and restore our religious liberty.

- **The Witherspoon Institute** (www.winst.org) in addition to providing research on religious liberty (in addition to other issues) publishes *Public Discourse*, an online journal that regularly provides scholarly articles about religious liberty.

Take a Stand for Religious Liberty

Dr. Philip Jenkins of Baylor University has called Catholic-bashing "American's last acceptable prejudice," though evangelical Protestants certainly get their fair share of bashing as well. Only Christian groups have been singled out at Hastings School of Law and Vanderbilt for special prejudicial treatment. Crosses, not giant Buddhas, are the subjects of lawsuits resulting in court orders to remove them from public view. This happened recently in the case of the cross on Mount Soledad near San Diego. The cross, placed there to honor military veterans, was too Christian and thus too offensive.

Some Christians might quote the words of Jesus in Matthew 5:38-39: "You have heard that it was said, 'An eye for an eye and a tooth for a tooth.' But I say to you, offer no resistance to one who is evil. When someone strikes you on your right cheek, turn the other one to him as well." Certainly there are occasions where it is right and good to simply permit ourselves to be abused for the sake of the Gospel.

Yet the Apostle Paul, when he was about to be flogged by Roman troops in Jerusalem, asked, "Is it lawful for you to scourge a man who is a Roman citizen and has not been tried?" (Acts 22:25). St. Paul asserted his rights as a Roman citizen and avoided the lash. Later, unhappy with the results of his trial, he again asserted his rights as a Roman citizen and appealed his case to Caesar (Acts 25:21).

You have rights including the right to the free exercise of religion. If the government is in some way abridging that right, take legal action. That's true for individuals, corporations, nonprofits, and churches.

If you or someone you know is being denied religious liberty, don't hesitate to contact the Thomas More Law Center, Alliance Defending Freedom, Liberty Counsel, the Becket Fund, or some other public interest law firm. These groups represent people of all faiths and *pro bono* help is available. They can evaluate whether or not you have a case and provide legal counsel if you do.

Getting involved is a matter of love for neighbor. As we've seen, whittling down anyone's religious freedom makes it that much easier to whittle away everyone's religious freedom. There may come a time when all we can do is turn the other cheek, but that time has not yet arrived. Those who wish to turn the Bill of Rights upside-down should not be permitted to have their way without a fight.

Evangelization

The last great persecution of Christians by the Roman Empire occurred in the early years of the fourth century. It was brutal and many Christian were martyred, but by that time, persecution to eradicate or even suppress the Church was an exercise in futility. As Church historian Robert Louis Wilken writes:

> Christians were too numerous, their communities too cohesive and organized, and their leaders too adroit to be done in by the sword. By forcing a choice between Rome and Christianity, the emperors badly misjudged the strength and resiliency of the Church. There was little popular support for the policy, and some citizens actually shielded Christians. [Persecuting Emperors] Diocletian and Galerius

represented a narrow and hard paganism that was divorced from the social fact that Christians were not outsiders but neighbors, friends, members of one's family, shopkeepers from whom one bought bread or vegetables or fish.[7]

The early Church was tightly knit, mission-focused, and evangelistic. Too often our parishes today are individualistic, unclear on the mission, and ingrown. A priest I know complains that most parishes have a franchise mentality: build it and they will come. While that may have been true once, he insists, those days are gone. Catholics are the largest Christian group in the country. The second largest group is lapsed Catholics who have either joined evangelical churches or the ranks of the unchurched.

Pope Francis addressed our need to evangelize in his Apostolic Exortation *Evangelii Gaudium* (*The Joy of the Gospel*):

> John Paul II asked us to recognize that "there must be no lessening of the impetus to preach the Gospel" to those who are far from Christ, "because this is the first task of the Church." Indeed, "today missionary activity still represents the greatest challenge for the Church" and "the missionary task must remain foremost." What would happen if we were to take these words seriously? We would realize that missionary outreach is paradigmatic for all the Church's activity.[8]

Evangelization, properly understood, does not "impose" our beliefs on others. Instead we *propose* the Gospel lovingly, graciously, respectfully, and winsomely through words and deeds. This is the kind of evangelization St. John Paul II, Benedict XVI, Francis, and countless other bishops encourage.

It can still provoke hatred, but more often it builds friendships and attracts people to Christ and his Bride, the Church.

Is it possible to turn a culture where Catholic-bashing and Christian-bashing are acceptable prejudices into a culture where bashing religious believers of any sort and denying anyone religious liberty is viewed as the work of the most narrow and hardened secularism, something unacceptable in polite society? I don't know and I certainly don't know what the future holds for the United States. But I agree with Benedict XVI that "The Gospel proclamation remains the first service that the Church owes to humanity in order to offer Christ's salvation to the people of our time, in so many ways humiliated and oppressed, and to give a Christian orientation to the cultural, social and ethical changes that are taking place in the world."[9]

If we are faithful "to offer Christ's salvation" and "to give a Christian orientation" to the world around us, God may well use our efforts as individuals, parishes, and dioceses for the advancement of religious liberty, Christian morality, and the Catholic faith.

Suffering

The story of religious liberty in the last number of years, along with the suffering of our brothers and sisters around the world, is a clear indication that Jesus' words, "In the world you will have trouble," (John 16:33) are true. Now the next word is "but" and we will get to the rest of Jesus' sentence, but let's begin by hearing these first words.

Yes, we should stand our ground and assert our rights as citizens. Yes, we should evangelize. Yes, we should pray. But in the final analysis, we may be called upon to suffer for the cause of Christ in an era that no longer tolerates the faith convictions of those whose faith, as someone put it, "has not petrified into politics and social service."

Francis Cardinal George, Archbishop of Chicago, has said, "I expect to die in bed, my successor will die in prison and his successor will die a martyr in the public square. . . . His successor will pick up the shards of a ruined society and slowly help rebuild civilization, as the church has done so often in human history."[10]

"In this world you will have trouble," said Jesus. He had trouble, the apostles had trouble, St. Cyprian and other early Christians had trouble, and believers around the world today are having great trouble and tribulation. We may join them in suffering. But Jesus didn't stop with trouble. He went on, "In this world you will have trouble, but take courage, I have conquered the world" (John 16:33).

Prayer

We take courage by praying alongside Jesus. We will do that when we understand three truths.

First, as St. Paul wrote, "For our struggle is not with flesh and blood but with the principalities, with the powers, with the world rulers of this present darkness, with the evil spirits in the heavens" (Ephesians 6:12). There is more at work in the battle for religious liberty than this world's politics. Spiritual enemies require spiritual armor and spiritual weapons. We have to pray for the devil's defeat.

2. Second, Jesus calls us to pray for our enemies, for those who hate us, and even for those who persecute us. Compromising religious liberty hurts everyone, and love for neighbor demands that we pray for those who oppose us and those who we oppose.

3. Third, St. Paul's admonition applies to us: "First of all, then, I ask that supplications, prayers, petitions, and thanksgivings be offered for everyone, for kings and for all in authority, that we may lead a quiet and tranquil life in all devotion and dignity. This is good and pleasing to God our savior, who wills everyone to be saved and to come to knowledge of the truth" (1 Timothy 2:1-4).

Our citizenship is in Heaven, but as long as we are here, God calls us to work and pray for the good of the world and the good of the nation into which he has seen fit to place us. We should pray, for example, that Cardinal George's dire prediction is dead wrong and that religious liberty will be restored rather than eroded.

Finally, in the shadow of the threats to our religious liberty, we do well to remember the words St. Teresa of Avila wrote in her Breviary:

Let nothing upset you;
Let nothing frighten you.
Everything is changing;
God alone is changeless.
Patience attains the goal.
Who has God lacks nothing;
God alone fills every need.[11]

AFTERWORD

Just a Pinch of Incense

IT is always, in every way and everywhere easier to go with the flow than to swim against it. But then again, as a friend likes to say, even a dead fish can float downstream. In third century North Africa, going with the flow by offering a pinch of incense to Roman gods was easy. After all, everyone else was doing it. To refuse out of Christian conviction as St. Cyprian did took—and still takes—heroic virtue.

Fr. George Rutler writes in his book, *A Crisis of Saints: The Call to Heroic Faith in an Unheroic World,* "All I really have to say about this is that each turning point in history is a test of holiness, and the saints make the big difference in the world's fortunes. As a corollary to this, since holiness is marked by heroic virtue, the real danger to society is not merely a lack of virtue, but lack of heroism."[1]

At this turning point, may God make us men and women who are marked by holiness, virtue, and heroism as together we face and fight the liberty threat.

Notes

Chapter 1—Ancient Christian Roots

I am particularly indebted to Robert Louis Wilken's book *The First Thousand Years: A Global History of Christianity.* It was Wilken who introduced me to the story of St. Cyprian and the details of the Edict of Milan.

1. "The Confession and Martyrdom of St. Cyprian, from the Proconsular Acts" in *A Library of Fathers of the Holy Catholic Church, Anterior to the Division of the East and West, Vol. III.* trans. Members of the English Church, (Oxford: James Parker & Co. and Rivingtons, 1839), xxv-xxix, https://archive.org/stream/a566167501cypruoft#page/n5/mode/2up.

2. *Ibid.*

3. *Tertullianus, Quintas Septimus Florens* (Tertullian), "To Scapula," trans. The Rev. S. Thelwall, in *Ante-Nicene Fathers, Vol. 3, Latin Christianity: Its Founder, Tertullian,* ed. Allan Menzies (Edinburgh: T & T Clark, 1996), 105-108, http://www.

ccel.org/ccel/schaff/anf03.iv.vii.i.html.

4. Thomas Jefferson, *Notes on the State of Virginia,* (Boston: Wells and Lilly, 1829), 166, https://ar chive.org/stream/notesonstateofvi00jeff/noteson stateofvi00jeff_djvu.txt.

5. Lucius Lactantius, "*Divine Institutes* on Defending True Religion through Faith, Not Force" (c. 308-309 CE), Berkley Center for Religion, Peace & World Affairs, http://berkleycenter.georgetown. edu/resources/quotes/lucius-lactantius-em-divine-institutes-em-on-defending-true-religion-through-faith-not-force-c-308-309-ce?q=.

6. Lactantius.

7. Constantine Augustus and Licinius Augustus, "The Edict of Milan," trans. University of Pennsylvania. Dept. of History: Translations and Reprints from the Original Sources of European History, Vol 4, (Philadelphia: University of Pennsylvania Press, 1897-1907)28-30, http://www. fordham.edu/halsall/source/edict-milan.asp.

8. Constantine Augustus and Licinius Augustus.

9. Second Vatican Council, *Dignitatis Humanae* [Declaration on Religious Freedom], 7 Dec. 1965, sec. 1, http://www.vatican.va/archive/ hist_councils/ii_vatican_council/documents/vat-ii_decl_19651207_dignitatis-humanae_en.html.

10. *Dignitatis Humanae*, sec. 5.

Chapter 2—Sweet Land of Liberty

In this chapter about the Colonial Era and founding of the United States, I am particularly indebted to Kevin Seamus Hasson's book *The Right to Be Wrong: Ending the Culture War Over Religion in America* and to Daniel Dreisbach and Mark David Hall, editors of *The Sacred Rights of Conscience: Selected Readings on Liberty and Church-State Relations in the American Founding* (Indianapolis: Liberty Fund, 2009).

1. Roger Williams, "To the Town of Providence," January 1655, http://press-pubs.uchicago.edu/founders/documents/amendI_religions6.html.

2. Monica Duffy Toft, Daniel Philpott, Timothy Samuel Shah, *God's Century: Resurgent Religion and Global Politics* (New York, London: W. W. Norton & Co., 2011), 220.

3. Kevin Seamus Hasson, *The Right to Be Wrong: Ending the Culture War Over Religion in America* (San Francisco: Encounter Books, 2005), 57.

4. Toleration Act of 1689 in *Statutes of the Realm, Vol. 6: 1685-94*, ed. John Raithby (London: unknown, 1819), 74-76, http://www.british-history.ac.uk/report.aspx?compid=46304.

5. *Order Book of Orange County, Virginia 1769-1777 287 (Oct. 28, 1773)* quoted in Andy G. Olree, "'Pride Ignorance and Knavery': James Madison's

Formative Experiences with Religious Establishments" in *Harvard Journal of Law & Public Policy,* 36, no. 1 (Winter 2012), 241.

6. Thomas Jefferson, Letter to William Short, 13 Apr. 1820, quoted in Hasson, 90.

7. Thomas Jefferson, Letter to James Madison, 15 Mar. 1789, quoted in Hasson, 96.

Chapter 3—We Hold These Truths

The discussion in this chapter owes a great deal to Daniel Dreisbach and his book *Thomas Jefferson and the Wall of Separation Between Church and State and to* David Sehat's *The Myth of American Religious Freedom.*

1. Paul Johnson, *A History of the American People* (New York: HarperCollins, 1997), 303.

2. David Sehat's *The Myth of American Religious Freedom* (Oxford: Oxford University Press, 2011), 158 and Pope Gregory XVI, *Mirari Vos* [Encyclical on Liberalism and Religious Indifferentism], August 15, 1832, http://www.papalencyclicals.net/Greg16/g16mirar.htm.

3. Daniel Dreisbach, *Thomas Jefferson and the Wall of Separation Between Church and State* (New York: New York University Press, 2002), 19.

4. Dreisbach, 9-17.

5. Address of the Danbury Baptist Association to

Jefferson, 7 Oct. 1808, in Dreisbach, 142-143.

6. Letter of Thomas Jefferson to the Danbury Baptist Association, 1 Jan. 1802 in Dreisbach 148.

7. United States Supreme Court, *Reynolds v. United States* (1879), quoted in Hasson, 102.

8. United States Supreme Court, *Reynolds v. United States* (1879), http://scholar.google.com/schol ar_case?case=1104642225155375579&hl=en& as_sdt=6&as_vis=1&oi=scholarr.

9. Michael McLean, "Statement Regarding Hobby Lobby Decision," Email, 30 Jun. 2014.

10. Jordan Lorance, conversation with author, date unknown.

11. Dreisbach, 103.

Chapter 4—Storm Clouds Gathering

In this chapter about the clear and present dangers to our religious liberty, I am especially indebted to my friends at The Catholic League, The Becket Fund, Alliance Defending Freedom, The Heritage Foundation, The Chaplain Alliance for Religious Liberty, and others who carefully report and/or litigate violations of religious liberty. In addition, I am grateful for publications such as *First Things, Touchstone, World, and Public Discourse.*

1. William Saunders, "The First Freedom: Why Religions Must Be Free, Not Tolerated," *Touchstone,*

April 2008, http://www.touchstonemag.com/ar chives/article.php?id=21-03-018-f.

2. Saunders.

3. The Becket Fund, Belmont Abbey College (2009), http://www.becketfund.org/bac09/.

4. *Ibid.*

5. Executive Order 13535, "Patient Protection and Affordable Care Act's Consistency with Long-standing Restrictions on the Use of Federal Funds for Abortion," 24 Mar. 2010, http://www. whitehouse.gov/the-press-office/executive-order-patient-protection-and-affordable-care-acts-con-sistency-with-longst.

6. Rep. Jeff Fortenberry quoted in Kathryn Jean Lopez, "Conscience Be Damned; the Obama Administration Makes HHS Rule Final," *National Review Online*, 28 Jan. 2013, http://m.nationalre-view.com/corner/352338/conscience-be-damned-obama-administration-makes-hhs-rule-final-kathryn-jean-lopez.

7. Archbishop William Lori and Russell Moore, "Standing Together for Religious Freedom: An Open Letter to All Americans," 2 Jul. 2013, http:// www.usccb.org/news/2013/13-134.cfm.

8. *Ibid.*

9. Thomas Farr quoted in Joan Frawley Desmond, "HHS Secretary Sebelius: Church Groups Must Provide Contraception," *National Catholic Register*, 20 Jan. 2012, http://www.ncregister.com/daily-news/hhs-secretary-sebelius-church-groups-must-provide-contraception/.

10. Alliance Defending Freedom Communications Office, Press Release: "New 'hate crimes' law drives another nail into First Amendment's coffin," 28 Oct. 2009, http://www.adfmedia.org/News/PRDetail/3312.

11. Chai Feldblum quoted by Maggie Gallagher, "Banned in Boston: Part 2," CBS News, 8 May 2006, http://www.cbsnews.com/news/banned-in-boston-part-two/.

12. *Ibid.*

13. Eric H. Holder, "Letter from the Attorney General to Congress on Litigation Involving the Defense of Marriage Act," United States Department of Justice, 23 Feb. 2011, http://www.justice.gov/opa/pr/2011/February/11-ag-223.html.

14. Jim Campbell quoted by Kathryn Jean Lopez, "Will Religious Liberty Survive Same-Sex Marriage?" *National Review Online*, 23 Aug. 2013, http://www.nationalreview.com/corner/356560/will-religious-liberty-survive-same-sex-marriage-kathryn-jean-lopez.

15. Hadley Arkes, "Judge Walker and the Language of the Law," *TheCatholicThing*, 16 Aug. 2010, http://www.thecatholicthing.org/columns/2010/judge-walker-and-the-language-of-the-law.html.

16. Alliance Defending Freedom Communications Office, Press Release: "Kansas school bans fliers with Bible verses," 2 Dec. 2013, http://www.adfmedia.org/News/PRDetail/8691.

17. Heather Clark, "Kansas School District Sued After Middle School Student Banned From Posting Bible Verses," *Christian News*, 3 Dec. 2013, http://christiannews.net/2013/12/03/kansas-school-district-sued-after-middle-school-student-banned-from-posting-bible-verses/.

18. PBS Religion & Ethics Newsweekly, "Christian Legal Society v. Martinez," 16 Apr. 2010, http://www.pbs.org/wnet/religionandethics/2010/04/16/april-16-2010-christian-legal-society-v-martinez/6109/.

19. *Ibid.*

20. *Ibid.*

21. George Washington, General Orders, 9 Jul. 1776, http://www.beliefnet.com/resourcelib/docs/108/George_Washington_General_Orders_July_09_1776_1p.html.

22. Archbishop Timothy P. Broglio, "Renewed Fideli-

ty in favor of Evangelization," Archdiocese for the Military Services, USA, 17 Sep. 2013, http://www. milarch.org/atf/cf/%7B1AF42501-01D5-4EF8-BA48-4450AC27EF98%7D/Renewed-Fidelity-in-favor-of-Evangelization-18SEP13.pdf.

23. Executive Office of the President, Office of Management and Budget, "Statement of Administrative Policy: HR 1960—National Defense Authorization Act for 2014," 11 June 2013, http://www. whitehouse.gov/sites/default/files/omb/legisla tive/sap/113/saphr1960r_20130611.pdf.

24. Vandenberg Air Force Base, "Visitor Information Package," no date, 4, http://www.vandenberg. af.mil/shared/media/document/AFD-110804-063.pdf.

25. Todd Starnes, "Air Force Suspends Christian-Themed Ethics Training Over Bible Passages," *Fox News*, 3 Aug. 2011, http://www.foxnews.com/pol-itics/2011/08/03/air-forces-suspends-christian-themed-ethics-training-program-over-bible/.

26. Nicola Menzie, "Evangelical Christianity, Catholicism Labeled 'Extremist' in Army Presentation," *The Christian Post*, 6 Apr. 2013, http://www. christianpost.com/news/evangelical-christianity-catholicism-labeled-extremist-in-army-presenta tion-93353/.

27. Geoff Herbert, "Air Force unit removes 'God'

from logo; lawmakers warn of 'dangerous precedent,'" *Syracuse.com*, 9 Feb. 2012, http://www.syracuse.com/news/index.ssf/2012/02/air_force_rco_removes_god_logo_patch.html.

28. Ben Burrows, "An Interview with Michael Weinstein," *The Philadelphia Jewish Voice*, Feb. 2008, http://www.pjvoice.com/v32/32300words.aspx.

29. Michael L. (Mikey) Weinstein, "Fundamentalist Christian Monsters: Papa's Got A Brand New Bag," *Huffington Post*, 16 Apr. 2013, http://www.huffingtonpost.com/michael-l-weinstein/funda mentalist-christian-_b_3072651.html.

30. William H. Brackney, "The Legacy of Adoniram Judson," International Bulletin of Missionary Research; Jul98, Vol. 22 Issue 3, p122, 6p, http://www.wmcarey.edu/carey/electronic-books/articles/legacy-judson.pdf.

Chapter 5—Reasserting Our Religious Liberty

In addition to the groups and publications mentioned in connection with Chapter 4, all of whom seek to reassert our religious liberty, I want to add the United States Conference of Catholic Bishops, The American Religious Freedom Program at the Ethics & Public Policy Center, and the Manhattan Declaration.

1. Augustine, *City of God,* trans. Marcus Dods, (New York: The Modern Library, 1950), 369.

2. Augustine, 3.

3. Richard John Neuhaus, "Iraq and the Moral Judgment," *First Things*, October 2005, http://www.firstthings.com/article/2005/10/iraq-and-the-moral-judgement.

4. Flannery O'Connor, "Some Aspects of the Grotesque in Southern Fiction," 1960, http://www.en.utexas.edu/amlit/amlitprivate/scans/grotesque.html.

5. "Declaration of the Rights of Man, 1789, Yale Law School Avalon Project, http://avalon.law.yale.edu/18th_century/rightsof.asp, article 10.

6. Randy Sly, "Obama Moves away from 'Freedom of Religion' toward 'Freedom of Worship'?" *Catholic Online*, 19 Jul. 2010, http://www.catholic.org/news/national/story.php?id=37390.

7. Robert Louis Wilken, *The First Thousand Years: A Global History of Christianity* (New Haven: Yale University Press, 2012), 78.

8. Pope Francis I, *Evangelii Gaudium* [Apostolic Exhortation on the Proclamation of the Gospel in Today's World], 24 Nov. 2013, http://w2.vatican.va/content/francesco/en/apost_exhortations/documents/papa-francesco_esortazione-ap_20131124_evangelii-gaudium.html, III.15.

9. Pope Benedict XVI, Angelus, 7 Oct. 2007, http://

www.vatican.va/holy_father/benedict_xvi/ange
lus/2007/documents/hf_ben-xvi_ang_20071007_
en.html.

10. Francis Cardinal George, "The Wrong Side
of History," *Catholic New World*, 3 Nov. 2012,
http://www.catholicnewworld.com/cnwon
line/2012/1021/cardinal.aspx.

11. Teresa of Avila, Prayer, https://www.ewtn.com/
Devotionals/prayers/StTeresaofAvila.htm.

Afterword

1. George W. Rutler, *A Crisis of Saints: The Call to
Heroic Faith in an Unheroic World* (New York:
The Crossroad Publishing Co., 2009), 2.

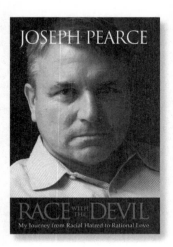

SAINT BENEDICT+PRESS

Saint Benedict Press publishes books, Bibles, and multimedia that explore and defend the Catholic intellectual tradition. Our mission is to present the truths of the Catholic faith in an attractive and accessible manner.

Founded in 2006, our name pays homage to the guiding influence of the Rule of Saint Benedict and the Benedictine monks of Belmont Abbey, just a short distance from our headquarters in Charlotte, NC.

Saint Benedict Press publishes under several imprints. Our TAN Books imprint (TANBooks.com), publishes over 500 titles in theology, spirituality, devotions, Church doctrine, history, and the Lives of the Saints. Our Catholic Courses imprint (CatholicCourses.com) publishes audio and video lectures from the world's best professors in Theology, Philosophy, Scripture, Literature and more.

For a free catalog, visit us online at
SaintBenedictPress.com

Or call us toll-free at
(800) 437-5876